The Complete Guide to
Building Affordable Earth-Sheltered Homes

Everything You Need to Know Explained Simply

By Robert McConkey

THE COMPLETE GUIDE TO BUILDING AFFORDABLE EARTH-SHELTERED HOMES: EVERYTHING YOU NEED TO KNOW EXPLAINED SIMPLY

Copyright © 2011 Atlantic Publishing Group, Inc.
1405 SW 6th Avenue • Ocala, Florida 34471 • Phone 800-814-1132 • Fax 352-622-1875
Web site: www.atlantic-pub.com • E-mail: sales@atlantic-pub.com
SAN Number: 268-1250

Library of Congress Cataloging-in-Publication Data

McConkey, Robert, 1956-
  The complete guide to building affordable earth-sheltered homes : everything you need to know explained simply / by Robert McConkey.
     p. cm.
  Includes bibliographical references and index.
  ISBN 978-1-60138-373-0 (alk. paper)
  1. Earth sheltered houses. I. Title.
  TH4819.E27M388 2010
  690'.8370473--dc22

                              2010028781

Printed in the United States

PROJECT MANAGER: Nicole Orr • PEER REVIEWER: Marilee Griffin • PROOFREADER: Katy Doll
INTERIOR DESIGN: Rhana Gittens • ASSISTANT EDITOR: Ben Stearns
FRONT COVER DESIGNER: Meg Buchner • meg@megbuchner.com
BACK COVER DESIGNER: Jackie Miller • millerjackiej@gmail.com

Cover Photo: Home of Mac & Lisa Moore, De Soto, WI

Printed on Recycled Paper

We recently lost our beloved pet "Bear," who was not only our best and dearest friend but also the "Vice President of Sunshine" here at Atlantic Publishing. He did not receive a salary but worked tirelessly 24 hours a day to please his parents. Bear was a rescue dog that turned around and showered myself, my wife, Sherri, his grandparents Jean, Bob, and Nancy, and every person and animal he met (maybe not rabbits) with friendship and love. He made a lot of people smile every day.

We wanted you to know that a portion of the profits of this book will be donated to The Humane Society of the United States. *–Douglas & Sherri Brown*

The human-animal bond is as old as human history. We cherish our animal companions for their unconditional affection and acceptance. We feel a thrill when we glimpse wild creatures in their natural habitat or in our own backyard.

Unfortunately, the human-animal bond has at times been weakened. Humans have exploited some animal species to the point of extinction.

The Humane Society of the United States makes a difference in the lives of animals here at home and worldwide. The HSUS is dedicated to creating a world where our relationship with animals is guided by compassion. We seek a truly humane society in which animals are respected for their intrinsic value, and where the human-animal bond is strong.

Want to help animals? We have plenty of suggestions. Adopt a pet from a local shelter, join The Humane Society and be a part of our work to help companion animals and wildlife. You will be funding our educational, legislative, investigative and outreach projects in the U.S. and across the globe.

Or perhaps you'd like to make a memorial donation in honor of a pet, friend or relative? You can through our Kindred Spirits program. And if you'd like to contribute in a more structured way, our Planned Giving Office has suggestions about estate planning, annuities, and even gifts of stock that avoid capital gains taxes.

Maybe you have land that you would like to preserve as a lasting habitat for wildlife. Our Wildlife Land Trust can help you. Perhaps the land you want to share is a backyard— that's enough. Our Urban Wildlife Sanctuary Program will show you how to create a habitat for your wild neighbors.

So you see, it's easy to help animals. And The HSUS is here to help.

2100 L Street NW • Washington, DC 20037 • 202-452-1100
www.hsus.org

Dedication

I would like to dedicate this book to my father, F. Paul McConkey, who has been a lifelong source of inspiration. As a frustrated homebuilder himself, he taught me that your home is always where your heart is.

Table of Contents

Chapter 4: The Good Earth — Site Development for an Earth-Sheltered Home   109

Chapter 5: On a Firm Foundation — Footing and Foundation Construction for an Earth-Sheltered Home 119

Chapter 6: Wired for Success – Installing Your Utilities 143

Chapter 9: The Icing on the Cake: Finishes and Amenities   231

Chapter 10: Home Sweet Home – What to Expect Living in an Earth-sheltered Home   253

Appendix A: Sample Material List   261

Appendix B: Typical Home Design Plan   263

Appendix C: Sample Construction Contract   265

Glossary   275

Bibliography   281

Author Biography   285

Index   287

Foreword

Chthonic. (thon'ik) The first time I saw this word I thought it was a new comic book super hero. Chthonic actually dates back to classical mythology and refers to beings that dwell under the earth. I am chthonic! In fact, for 28 years now, I have been a part of a unique chthonic culture.

In a way, most chthonic individuals have to be strong willed because, in spurning conventional housing and choosing to live underground, they have selected a lifestyle that goes against tradition. In 1982, when the plans for my 3,000-square-foot underground home went through the zoning and building permit boards in Platte County, Missouri, there was some controversy over the proposed building. Not only was it the first such proposal in our county, but a recent tragedy involving a collapsed building in Kansas City had already made people in the area nervous about construction methods. The controversy came not only from the regulatory boards but also from family, friends, and even strangers. Yet, being the stubborn person that I am, the opposition only proved inspiring to me as I vowed to be strong and true to my belief and dream of an energy-efficient, disaster-safe, and cost-effective home for my family.

Choosing to live underground is not a one-and-done type of choice. An earth-sheltered life is a life defined by a number of choices. It did not take long for me to begin to recognize and appreciate the many blessings this lifestyle brought to our family. I found myself free of conventional comparisons. Our indoor slide actually became the envy of my children's friends. I have always loved and appreciated the environment, but living in an earth-sheltered home brought me even closer to nature. I found myself stopping to look a little longer at the sunsets, the ever-changing vegetation, and the entertaining wildlife that seemed less afraid of me and my home than in other, more traditional settings. With concrete and steel beams underneath 3 feet of dirt and grass and over my head, I feel much safer than I ever have in other homes. Ice storms breaking large limbs or toppling entire trees would simply bring them to rest on our grass roof. Even a fire could not destroy the basic concrete foundation. Although tornados could possibly destroy our aboveground garages, they could not endanger us below. With our wood burning stove, should storms knock out the power, we can still stay warm, cook hot meals, dry wet clothing, and provide shelter and warmth for others as well.

Somewhere along the way, while living underground, I realized that I had begun to value simplicity more and more. This left me with more free time to be creative, and I was happier. I loved to hear the knocking of my children on the skylight above the kitchen when they wanted to know how long until dinner. To be able to look up at those smiling, sometimes dirty, little faces continually energized me. As a family, we learned to enjoy our unique living situation, and I believe it helped all of us learn to care less about what others think and more about what we think of ourselves.

I remember an elderly washer repairman trudging up our 18 stairs to the garage exit, and, when he reached the top, he turned around and shyly started to ask if, maybe, he could...

"Try the slide?" I finished for him.

His boyish grin as he came down that slide still brings a smile to my face.

Living under the earth has not only helped me develop my sense of humor, but it has become an essential sixth sense in my life. The first few years after we moved into our earth-sheltered home, our electric company would send out meter readers on a regular basis to check our suspiciously low meter readings. Now, they finally get it! Once, I received a soliciting phone call for a furnace check-up. I politely told the man we did not have a furnace, only to have him gruffly demand, "Lady, let me talk to your husband!"

As with the building of any home, careful planning, research, and qualified, experienced builders will help to prevent major problems. Little problems are a part of every life, so do not sweat them. I will always be thankful for our builder, Riley Brown, a concrete specialist who was way ahead of his time. Not only was he living in an underground home he had built, but his grown children and grandchildren were also living in one that he had built. That was the deal clincher for me.

I hope I can follow the example of my home and rise to my fullest potential in extreme situations, because that is when its worth truly shines. And that is when people knock on our door asking to be put on the list of interested parties in case we ever decide to sell.

Robert Frost once said, "I shall be telling this with a sigh, somewhere ages and ages hence: Two roads diverged in a wood, and I took the one less traveled by, and that has made all the difference."

This book has the potential to make all the difference for you and your life. And if it does, I truly hope our chthonic paths may someday cross.

Cathy Runyan Svacina

Introduction

"God owns heaven but he craves the earth"
— Anne Sexton, American poet

I first became interested in earth-sheltered homes after visiting a full-scale model of a Native American (First Nation) earth shelter at the natural history museum in Vancouver, British Columbia. This intriguing underground home was made of beams, branches, and bark with an earth cover. It was used by coastal Indian tribes in the Pacific Northwest as a simple family home. Known as a pit-home because it is built into a covered pit, this unique shelter caught my attention for its simplicity and functionality. Elegantly constructed over an excavated bowl of earth, it had a central, peaked opening for smoke to exit and to allow access via

Pit home photo courtesy of Helen McConkey

a ladder. Nestled comfortably in this fire heated-pit, a native family could sleep, play, eat, and work.

This structure made me think seriously for the first time about the true utility of using the earth as a building material. I could not help but imagine a family huddled comfortably here through the bitter Northwest winter storms. The graceful design seems so well-adapted to its use. I also could not help but think about how different it was from my current, modern house. The cold, angular designs of modern homes seem to miss something important in their design. Using the earth seems to add an element of warmth to modern structures. The natural harmony of this type of shelter intrigued me. I found myself wondering if there was a way to blend the conveniences of a contemporary residence with the order and comfort of this type of native earth-shelter. Using readily available natural materials, these homes made perfect sense. The harmony between the structure and the earth around it seem much more like the way nature intended it to be. These types of homes seemed far more practical than the wood plank, long houses that Northwest Native American tribes are known for.

Earth-sheltered housing came to a modern resurgence in America in the 1970s and early 1980s with a greater public consciousness about protecting the environment and saving energy. The trend still seems to be continuing. With fuel costs rising and a renewed interest in getting back to nature, people have started turning to the earth for answers. Affordability and sustainability have become big issues. Earth-sheltered construction seemed like the best way to save energy and resources and to create a simple, more practical type of home.

Of course, using the earth as a shelter is nothing new. Cave dwellers in early human history knew the advantages of using the earth for protection from the elements. For one thing, it was extremely inexpensive to find a natural cave and heat it with a fire. In this way, an earth home provided practical and simple protection from the elements. Sheltered by the earth, this type of living provided excellent protection from the weather, natural disasters, and even wild animals. This type of shelter was also easy to maintain as long as you did not have to compete with other animals for your living space. For these reasons, earth-sheltering was a very common way of living in the past. Almost every Native American group had developed their own type of earth-sheltered home, found almost everywhere from the Navajo's adobe "Hogan's" to the cliff houses of the Mesa Verde. All had learned how to efficiently use the earth to make a home. Even the American pioneers used earth-sheltering techniques as they migrated across the United States. What made these homes so appealing and why were they such an important part of our past?

Like everything else, earth-sheltered living has come a long way since the days of the early shelter builders. Modern technology has made underground living even more efficient and practical. Modern building techniques and materials offer a wide range of possibilities never imagined by early shelter builders. For some, earth-sheltered homes have even become a desired luxury. Modern building science has not only enhanced the process of earth-shelter construction, it has made it more affordable and aesthetically pleasing.

As a homebuilder and national director for the Kitsap County Home Builders Association in Washington State, I have followed with great interest the natural progression of earth-sheltered buildings for many years. In the course of the last few decades, there have been remarkable advances in the structural design, water-proofing technologies, and finishes for underground homes. Architects experimenting with underground construction have created remarkable examples of what can be done using the earth as a building material. Underground construction has been used to build homes, public schools, libraries, and shopping malls.

Owners and builders pushing the envelope with new materials and construction techniques have created a broad range of options. Many homebuilders have even decided to become specialized in this type of building. Some even travel the country as they help many find the joys of living underground.

As a practical and simple guide to affordable underground construction, this book is a step-by-step approach to building a cost-effective, earth-sheltered home. In the book, you will find tips and ideas for researching, planning, and building an affordable earth-sheltered home. The book was designed for both the curious and the committed; for those curious about underground housing, it is a good place to explore, and for those committed to actually building their own underground house, it is a good place to start.

A wealth of information is continuously updated both in print and online. Some of this valuable knowledge is still not widely dispersed. Other ideas are so new they are still being played with. For owners and builders, this book is full of practical information from planning to the final key turning of a home. As earth-sheltered homes are compared to their conventional counterparts, the differences will be revealed, and it may be enough to persuade those who were just looking to read more about an underground home to actually build one. Furthermore, this book examines how to make your house more affordable at each step of the building process, because it even explains how to predict and control your construction costs. You will find case studies with advice from underground housing experts for common construction tips and ideas, and you should come away with an appreciation for earth-sheltered homes and why underground housing has a very bright future in the home building industry of tomorrow.

Chapter 1

Earth-Sheltered Housing:
The Good, the Bad, and the Ugly

> *"We do not inherit the earth from our fathers. We borrow it from our children."*
>
> — *David Brower, 20th Century environmentalist*

The Benefits of Earth-Sheltered Housing

One of the first things I discovered about earth-sheltered homes is that there is more than one kind. In a liberal sense, the definition includes everything from converted intercontinental ballistic missile (ICBM) shelters, to homes constructed of earth-filled bags. There are even underground homes that have been constructed of geodesic domes or converted mine shafts. The wide range of different types of earth-sheltered homes leads to much confusion. The average person, after hearing the term "earth-sheltered home," usually has to stop and think a bit about what the term means. In fact, I have found that every person seems to have a different mental picture.

In simple terms, an earth-sheltered home is a residence construct-ed with an earth covering for its roof or walls. Earth-sheltered homes are also sometimes called "underground homes," but this name is not very descriptive. Most underground homes are not totally underground — they are just covered with earth. It is pos-sible to have an earth-sheltered home with bermed walls totally above the ground. In modern literature, these structures can con-sist of almost anything from a simple cave carved into the side of a cliff to a cottage constructed of rammed earth. Perhaps one of the most famous examples can be found in JRR Tolkien's *The Hob-bit* — the hobbit hole that tunnels into the side of a hill. The key distinction in earth-sheltered construction is the use of earth as an integral part of the structure. But, why would someone want to actually build or live in one?

What makes these homes different from conventional homes? Are they any better than regular homes? These are all good ques-tions. The most powerful answers come from those who have built their own underground homes.

For the owners and builders who are just starting out, an earth-sheltered home represents an adventure. For the builder who specializes in underground homes, the homes have come to mean more than just an alternate style of home building. For both, un-derground homes seem to have become more of a lifestyle than a type of construction. Many earth–sheltered homebuilders started building these structures as their first homes. Attracted to the initial idea of an underground home, they were the ones to first see the benefits. Learning by trial and error, these pioneers of the industry are the ones who have helped earth-sheltered homes in-crease in popularity. Some of these builders could not keep from helping others build their own underground homes, enamored by the benefits of using the earth's natural resources for construction. I have to admit, the enthusiasm of these builders seems contagious, and it turns out the passion of earth shelter builders was not misplaced. Earth-sheltered homes do have significant advantages over conventionally constructed homes, the first and most important of these being their cost.

Affordable earth shelters

In an age when the costs of housing are escalating out of control, earth-sheltered homes have become an attractive alternative. As wood becomes more expensive, the price of earth looks much more reasonable. This is the logic that most people follow and sometimes it works. Earth-sheltered homes can be constructed on a unit-cost basis that is much more affordable than conventional construction. The emphasis here, however, is on the word "can," because earth-sheltered homes can also be more expensive. Typical unit costs for a single family home in the Pacific Northwest now run about $75 per square foot of finished construction. Earth-sheltered homes can be reasonably built anywhere from $40 to $95 per square foot.

Building costs vary greatly depending on the materials used and what must be done both structurally and architecturally. Because of the many differences, comparing the cost of earth-sheltered construction to conventional construction is sometimes difficult. It is sometimes like the old exercise of comparing apples to oranges or, in this case, maybe wood to dirt. Cost information can be very confusing. Some custom shelter builders say confidently that earth shelters cost 15 to 20 percent more than conventional housing designs. Other owners or builders often quote prices 20 to 30 percent less. The difference seems to stem from whom you are getting your information and what types of costs the person sees. The facts, when carefully examined, show that three things are important to any housing cost:

1. The complexity of the house design

2. The types of materials used

3. Whether or not the owner takes part in the construction process

For complex houses designed by a specialty architect and built by a custom homebuilder, the costs for earth-sheltered homes can greatly exceed conventional construction. Custom designs add cost not only in the design but in the actual construction process. Custom-designed houses are always more expensive than stock plan designs and can be 20 to 2,000 percent more, depending on the types of customizations. Someone once said that "good architecture is waste," which is true to a certain extent. A good architect can add plenty of expense to a project just by adding materials that have an expensive look. Complex and expensive architectural features, such as domed ceilings, fancy skylights, Corian countertops, and vertical grain Douglas fir doors can add expense to any home.

It is so difficult to pin down the cost of a custom home because architects can add expensive and exotic materials that add large, additional expense to the structure. The types of things that one sees in extremely expensive custom homes include complex ar-chitectural features, like domed ceilings. Dome ceilings can be constructed out of wood or concrete but are costly to engineer and build. One common practice in building custom homes today is to build elevated ceilings that are nine or 10 feet high instead of the traditional 8-foot ceilings. These elevated ceilings require more material to frame and more material to cover the additional area. Other expensive amenities, such as high-end woods, plumbing fixtures, light fixtures, and exotic finishes can add expense to a home structure based on proportion to the square-footage costs of the building. One has only to look at the type of amenities found in the homes of the rich and famous to see how a custom home's cost can escalate through the roof.

Custom building also costs more to construct. A typical custom builder marks up his or her project 15 to 20 prevent higher than normal tract homebuilders. This extra cost is added because custom homes are harder to build, take longer to finish, and require more planning and expertise to build. The average small homebuilder can build eight to ten stock homes in a year, whereas a custom homebuilder might build only two. Custom homebuilders must allot the same amount of overhead from eight houses to two to stay in business. Most earth-sheltered homebuilders fall in the category of custom builders because of the specialized nature of this type of work. This is not to say, however, that using custom architects and builders is not worth the extra cost — you just need to be aware that you are paying for it.

The unique nature of underground construction can also add structural costs to your project. Typical underground homes have a roof cover somewhere between 6 inches and 4 feet. A 4-foot roof covering obviously requires much more structural strength than a 6-inch covering. The heavier the earth cover, the more money you will have to spend on the support structure for your roof, meaning it will be bigger or thicker. At some point, there is an economical break-even point where more cover does not provide any more advantages for the cost expenditure. A general rule is that most of the advantages of an earth shelter are found in the first 8 to 10 inches of cover. These advantages are lost after 1 to 2 feet of cover. Therefore, covering with more than 3 feet makes no sense from a cost standpoint.

Though expensive designs and custom builders can add expense to your project, a simple design can save you money. Earth dwellings can be designed from something as simple as a cave in the side of a hill to an arched dome of earth bags. Significant amounts of money can be saved in the simplicity of the design. *This will be discussed in Chapter 3.*

The use of native materials for wall and roof covering or construction can also save money on structural components, siding, roofing, and other parts of the structure. Dirt is cheap and abundant, and when combined with other alternate materials, it can be very affordable. Using native and alternate materials offers many ways to save significant building expenses on the shell structure of an underground home. Though conventional homes are generally in the range of $65 to $75 per square foot for the building shell, reliable numbers for affordable earth shelter shells can be anywhere from $35 to $95 per square foot, depending on the methods and materials used for construction.

The use of owner labor, or what is known as "sweat equity" — a term that refers to the value added to a home or building by hard work or endeavors — is yet another way to make any type of housing more affordable. The labor part of a home construction can make up to half of a project's cost. By completing this labor themselves, owners or builders can save significant labor costs. One owner/builder interviewed for this book saved $66,000 on an $180,000 home in labor costs.

Simple designs, native or alternate materials, and owner labor can considerably change the cost picture. Earth-sheltered homes can be built more affordable than conventional homes. Because this book is about "affordable" earth-sheltered homes, this is obviously the emphasis. This book will explore ways to make a home more affordable at every step of the process. If saving money excites you, there are two other noteworthy ways in which earth-sheltered homes can make living more affordable. The first of these is the substantial savings in energy consumption.

Energy savings and temperature comfort

One advantage of earth-sheltered homes stands out above all of the others: They are much more energy efficient. Heating and cooling an underground home costs significantly less money than heating or cooling a home with conventional construction. This is an advantage that has appeal both for the cost conscious and the environmentally friendly. The energy efficiency of earth shelters makes them cheaper to heat during the winter and much cheaper to cool during the summer months. Less money spent on energy now means more energy for the future.

Energy Savings on an Earth-sheltered home	
Normal Heating Bill (Yearly)	Typical Savings with 75 percent more efficiency (for ten years)
$ 900	$ 6,750
$ 1200	$ 9,000
$ 1600	$ 12,000
$ 2200	$ 16,500

The property of earth-sheltered homes that makes them more energy efficient has long been thought by many to be the good insulation properties of earth. This is actually quite wrong. Earth is not a good insulator at all, but rather an extremely good conductor of heat. The insulation value of dirt compares to that of a rock, like granite. Earth conducts heat almost three times better than water, and 50 percent better than pure glass.

The R-value of a material is a measure of its thermal conductance; thus, different materials have different R-values based on how well they conduct heat. The higher the R-value, the better a material provides insulation. One inch of granite has an R-value near 1.0. Aerogel foam, one of the best insulators there is, has an R-value of 10.0. One inch of earth has an R-value very close to that of granite, about 1.0. Most insulation materials have much higher R-values. Extruded polystyrene foam has a published R-value of 5.0, which means that 1 inch of polystyrene insulation is roughly five times as good an insulator as 1 inch of earth. If earth is such a good conductor, what makes it so energy efficient?

The ability of earth to help with energy efficiency relies on two things: the first is called thermal mass, and the second is the almost universally constant temperature of the earth itself below the frost line. Thermal mass, also called thermal capacity or thermal capacitance, is the physical ability of a material to store or hold heat. The term thermal mass is used in building design to indicate the resistance of building materials to lose heat. The earth has a very high thermal mass, which means that once heated, it stores its heat well. Because you are relying on the earth and its thermal mass, earth-sheltered homes hold their heat longer once heated and lose their inherent heat slower. The earth surrounding the structure acts as a huge heat sink to stabilize temperature fluctuations.

Below the frost line of soil, the temperature of the earth anywhere on the earth is almost always a universal 50 to 60 degrees. This temperature never changes significantly from season to season regardless of where you are. This combination of extreme thermal stability with a constant year-round temperature makes the earth an excellent material to build against. This large storehouse of cool energy can be transferred to your home to make summertime cooling much easier. Instead of cooling your home from an outside temperature of 90 degrees, you are cooling it naturally by the flow of heat from the warm house to the cooler earth. Without any energy, it will remain a comfortable 70 degrees just from the house-to-earth heat transfer.

Even better than the energy savings from cooling your underground home are the energy savings you get from heating it — warming your house also requires less energy because of the earth's energy store. Instead of heating your home from an outside temperature of near freezing, you are heating it from an earth-stabilized inside temperature of about 55 degrees. Because of this, even a totally unheated underground house will never drop below 50 to 55 degrees. The thermal mass or storage capacity of the earth protects your home from extreme temperatures during both the summer and the winter. What this means is temperature comfort and extremely efficient energy savings in excess of 75 to 80 percent more than conventional housing. In hard money, this means someone who spends $1,400 per month to heat and cool his or her house is now spending only about $250 per month. Add these savings up over the life span of a typical house and you are talking major savings. Though conventional home temperatures fluctuate through heating and cooling cycles as the heater and air conditioner turn on and off, underground homes remain comfortable and cozy. This is a profound difference worth considering, especially when the costs for most forms of heating energy rise every year.

The extreme thermal storage capacity of earth also provides an excellent solution for passive solar heating or wood heating. The sun's warmth or a fire's heat can be collected during the day and released slowly over the nighttime hours. Because of this energy efficiency, earth-sheltered homes are considered an extremely green and sustainable technology. This has great appeal in an age when people are worried about the negative effects our civilization has on the world around us.

Energy savings can be significant in an earth-sheltered home. Careful scientific energy studies in Colorado have shown consistent and remarkable savings year-round. Aside from cost savings in construction and heating, a third, possibly more powerful, way to make living more affordable is offered through earth-sheltered housing — the savings in maintenance costs.

Maintenance savings

Much of the expense of a conventional home comes in the form of what is commonly known as costs of ownership. These are costs for which you cannot borrow money from a bank. They are usually huge, unbudgeted expenses that come at the most unexpected times. These costs are hard to plan for and are sometimes even harder to swallow. For example, a maintenance cost can occur after a rain storm when your roofer tells you it might be time for a new roof, or in the middle of the summer when your spouse casually mentions the house sure could use a fresh coat of paint. These costs are the direct results of sun, wind, and water decay on the outside structure of your home. They are the ever-present maintenance costs associated with maintaining the exterior of a home — regardless of what your home is built out of.

The exterior of a conventional home must be reroofed, re-sided, and repainted with periodic frequency or it will become unlivable. Average homes may have gutters to be cleaned or masonry fireplaces to be re-tucked, but underground homes require much less exterior maintenance. Dirt covers many areas that would traditionally have to be maintained. A roof covered by grass will not need to be reroofed, and an exterior wall covered with dirt will never have to be repainted. One of the greatest advantages to earth-sheltered homes is that you do not have to worry about these maintenance nightmares. Where conventional home roofing and siding must be replaced in 15- to 20-year cycles, turf construction can remain unmaintained for centuries. Likewise, conventional homes may need roofs repaired, but an underground home may just need the roof grass mowed.

Because of the minimal types of maintenance required, the maintenance costs of an earth-sheltered home are less than one-fourth of those of a conventional home. This is significant when the average home reroof is $15,000, and the cost increases daily. The general durability of an earth shelter is also considered a positive advantage in itself. Constructed of concrete and earth, the life span of underground homes is far greater than any conventional housing. Most conventional homes are torn down and remodeled or rebuilt after less than 100 years. The oldest earth shelters built in Scotland, on the other hand, are more than 5,000 years old. Conservative estimates for underground housing built with modern materials have projected life spans of 200 to 300 years. This means that a $200,000 conventional home must be replaced with a $500,000 home sometime in the future. An earth shelter of the same price will still be in good shape when its mortgage has been paid off, making the life cycle costs of an earth-sheltered home unbeatable.

Aside from significant savings in construction, energy consumption, and maintenance costs, earth-sheltered homes have many other attractive features. These are features that are not found in conventional-style homes.

CASE STUDY: LIFE CYCLE COSTS

Ralph Smoot
R.C. Smoot Construction
P.O. Box 1736
Bastrop, TX 78602
earthshelteredhome.com
rcsmoot@gmail.com
(512) 944-8820

In researching earth-sheltered housing, there is one source of information that seems to stand clearly above all the rest — that is the R. C. Smoot Construction company. Ralph Smoot, the original owner, has more than 27 years of experience building earth-sheltered homes and said that he someday plans to write a book on the subject himself. I can say with confidence that it will be a book well worth reading.

After 27 years of building earth-sheltered homes, Smoot's company has collected a wealth of experience and information about earth-sheltered homes. His website covers an encyclopedia of facts about all aspects of earth shelter construction from reasons to build, myths about them, and different styles of construction. For $25, you can even order a DVD from the website designed specifically for do-it-yourselfers.

On the phone, Ralph's voice undeniably exudes his enthusiasm for underground construction. His general philosophy seems to follow a line of reasoning that is hard to argue with. His main point is that earth-sheltered homes provide much better value than conventional homes. Besides taking only 25 percent of the energy cost to heat, the life cycle cost of an earth-sheltered home far exceeds its conventional counterpart. Undeniable evidence shows that earth-sheltered homes last longer and are less expensive to maintain than regular wood frame houses.

Where Ralph sees the big difference is after 15 to 17 years when a conventional home starts to break down. This is the point where underground homes become a great investment. He says that with solid construction, low maintenance, and energy efficiency, "more of your assets stay in savings instead of supporting a deteriorating wood frame." This is particularly true for older retired people who do not want to worry about getting hit with a huge maintenance expense when they can least afford it.

The R.C. Smoot Construction portfolio includes some very interesting projects. The project pictured here is of a structure in Denton County, Texas. It was built so strongly it can support a steel pyramid structure above its concrete underground superstructure.

As a leader in the industry, Ralph is not afraid to be innovative and explore new building technologies and techniques. Another design, called the California home "shell" construction, offers the company's first underground home designed for complete off-grid living.

As housing costs increase, many homes become more of a financial burden than an asset for their owners. Earth-sheltered homes offer an attractive alternative that everyone should consider. Exciting new building techniques and green sustainable building support rather than detract from the natural environment. That, according to Ralph, is what sustainable living and the future is all about.

Natural lighting

The most common misconception about underground houses is that they are damp, dark, and claustrophobic. If properly designed, however, underground homes can be just as comfortable as aboveground living. Most incorporate plenty of natural light, proper ventilation, and a good use of open space, causing many earth shelter dwellers to think it is one of the most comfortable ways to live. Modern underground designs usually include southern exposure with an internal atrium and courtyards that allow natural light to come from every direction. Additionally, better air handling in an earth shelter can create a dust and allergy-free environment.

A dust-free environment

Underground homes have fewer exterior wall penetrations to let air in from the outside. This translates to a tighter wall structure and has the advantage of reducing air infiltration that can bring with it dust and pollen. It also reduces convection heat losses through exterior wall airflow. This is a common problem in conventional structures. It is said that if you add up all the small wall cracks, in most modern-day homes, you would have an opening about the size of a small window. This is a window that would always be open to allow a constant flow of air to penetrate the house. Without these small cracks earth-sheltered homes have much less air flowing through them. This means less dust and allergens will be brought in from the outside.

Properly designed underground homes have also eliminated many of the water problems that plague basements in normal houses. Devised to eliminate water infiltration, underground homes are better suited to deal with water problems than regular basements that lack such planning.

A disaster-safe environment

When living in a home sheltered by the earth, there is a built-in protection from fire, storms, sound, and even radiation. Just 6 to 8 inches of earth can provide most of the benefits of this protection; therefore, earth-sheltered homes are much safer than conventional housing.

The use of fire-resistant materials makes an underground home virtually fire safe. Dirt does not burn, and most of the superstructure components found in earth shelters are also fire resistant. The types of materials used in earth shelters, such as concrete, metal, and masonry products, all have a high fire ratings that will protect a structure from fire for many hours.

The protective use of an earth cover can also provide foolproof protection from hurricanes, tornadoes, windstorms, hail, lighting, and earthquakes. There is no need to travel to a root cellar when the tornado comes, or to worry about lightening or hail damage to the exterior of your home during a storm. Shelter, by the earth's protection, is even offered while you sleep. Earth-sheltered homes are usually more resistant to earthquake damage than modern homes. A design that provides protection for an earth covering includes the proper engineering for structural movement of the earth. Sheltering by the earth makes it much harder for the elements to reach you.

In the worst-case scenario, earth shelters can even provide protection from nuclear calamity. Having your own personal fallout shelter is seen as a huge advantage in many of the survivalist communities in Southern Oregon and Idaho. One company in Kansas (**www.missilebases.com**) is even selling converted Atlas "F" Missile Base silos as underground survival condos for $900,000. Sheltered by an earth cover, underground homes can provide protection from blast damage and radiation.

One often-overlooked advantage of underground construction is sound protection. If you live near an airport or another noisy facility, it is a much-appreciated advantage. Earth coverings do an excellent job of attenuating and deadening sound from virtually any source. Patents have been issued for using the earth as a noise protection feature in the construction of schools and businesses that are next to airports, train stations, or highway noise.

Insurance benefits

Because of the disaster benefits of earth-sheltered construction, there are even insurance benefits from living underground. In speaking directly with a local home insurance agent, the price quoted for an earth-sheltered home was about five percent lower for two houses of equal value. Typical home insurance runs for $400 to $1,200, so a savings of even up to 10 percent is not a huge deal. But, every little bit helps.

Other advantages

Many other benefits of living underground can be found if you look hard enough at the differences. Everything from rodent and pest resistance to protection from burglar intrusion has been attributed to earth shelters. In some areas of the country, energy tax credits are even available for earth-sheltered home construction. One of the most interesting advantages I have heard about, however, was described by an architect as better lot utilization. He was able to make a building lot much more usable by designing a home with parking on the roof.

Probably one of the biggest advantages to underground living, however, is not so easily quantified: the unique lifestyle it affords those who adopt it.

A unique lifestyle

Earth-sheltered homes are a very different way to live — a way that is often hard to accurately portray. Shelter living is a lifestyle that involves living in total harmony with the earth. Tales of roof vegetable gardens or deer grazing on roof covers are found commonly in the literature about underground homes. Sharing one's life with the nurturing aspects of the earth seems to strike people on a primal level. Most people who live in earth-sheltered homes are extremely loyal to them. In fact, many who have adopted this lifestyle would never give it up.

From this high praise comes many remarkable testimonials. Ruth Davis, one earth-sheltered resident builder I spoke with, said she would never move under any circumstances, and if she had to move it would be to another earth-sheltered home. In some parts of the country and abroad, whole communities have grown up around earth-sheltered living, sharing the culture of sustainable and comfortable living together.

It seems that even when you add up all of the tangible benefits of underground living, there still remain many intangible ones that cannot be easily described. The simple, pure, and aesthetic benefits of life in harmony with nature seems to resonate with some deeper part of human nature and experience. It is something that makes this lifestyle appeal on a deep emotional level in and of itself.

The Disadvantages of Earth-Sheltered Living

All the talk about the advantages of earth-sheltered homes makes them seem quite appealing. Balance requires that this book also look at the disadvantages. No matter how perfect anything is, it is never without a downside. Even with the many benefits afforded by earth-sheltered living, there are still a few disadvantages that need to be considered.

Ironically, one of the earth shelter's biggest disadvantages comes from one of its greatest strengths; its uniqueness. Because this style of home construction is not considered conventional, it is still not widely accepted by the general public. Many still consider it an experimental method of homebuilding. Because of this, financing and marketing are often more difficult.

Mortgage problems

The biggest problem with earth-sheltered homes is sometimes just finding the money to build one. The size of this problem probably depends on where you live and the local market's general acceptance of underground homes. Earth-sheltered homes are getting more popular every day, but they are still not commonly built in the United States. A conventional mortgage company that has no experience with them is naturally going to be leery of loaning money on one. Lenders are more reserved when it comes to loaning conventional money on less conventional types of construction. The problem is not solely confined to earth-sheltered homes, but with any atypical type of home construction. The same challenges that have hindered the financing of Buckminster Fuller's geodesic dome home construction have hindered underground construction. In the housing market of 2009, most banks wrote mortgages with the intention of later selling them to secondary markets. To sell a mortgage, it must comply with long lists of federal government standards. Underground homes do not comply. Non-conventional types of construction, like earth-sheltered homes, cannot be guaranteed.

Another problem is that the value of earth homes is much harder to determine for financing purposes. This may be due to an inability of normal home appraisers to appraise them, or because not enough of them have been built to gather statistical information on their R-value. Because they cannot be valued properly, most conventional banks just exclude them.

A study in the United Kingdom looked at what it would take to get conventional lenders to lend on underground home designs. They were specifically interested in mass-produced underground home developments, so they sent a survey to lenders, most of whom said they would decline financing on any earth-sheltered type of construction. The reason they gave was that there was "no established data to validate the construction form," meaning that the problem is that without financing, the construction form cannot be validated. This type of Catch-22 leaves the earth-shelter builder without government support in an era when the government is encouraging energy-efficient design, but not helping to validate the design so that it can be loaned against.

A search for mortgage companies that will lend on earth-shelters shows that they do exist, but are still uncommon. Many, like the Earthlog Equity Group, specialize in all aspects of earth-shelter construction and offer financing as a way to sell more earth homes. The secret is to find a lender who has experience with earth-sheltered homes and who is not afraid of them. Custom earth-shelter builders often have lending lined up as a part of their building packages. This money is usually not much more expensive to borrow than conventional money but it is harder to find. Companies like Earthlog offer lending services on homes built anywhere in Canada, the United States, or Australia. The rates are slightly higher than conventional home loans, but are designed specifically for earth-sheltered construction.

Recent government financing trends are also improving daily. The government recently introduced conventional loan VA and FHA programs for underground homes, but financing on them is still considered a challenge. The VA is a loan from the Department of Veteran Affairs and is designed specifically for veterans, and FHA loans are from the Federal Housing Authority, which stands behind most federally insured home loans. Other avenues to pursue are the several government energy programs that certify homes by virtue of their energy efficiency. Though not very helpful on the more uncommon types for earth shelters, such certifications can be used to secure home loans through more conventional sources. Programs such as Zero Energy or Plus Energy Homes provide government-sponsored support for mortgages. Once a home's design meets the requirements of such a program, they are automatically insured by the government and can be financed through conventional sources.

Another option is to research the Energy Efficient Mortgage (EEM). This was a pilot mortgage program that was started in 1992 in five states and has since expanded to a national program. EEMs are designed so that energy savings in a home allow a home buyer to qualify for a larger loan than he or she could normally qualify for. This increase in the mortgage amount is secured by anticipated lower energy expenditures. The FHA's EEMs can run through a regular mortgage bank and are insured by the U.S. Department of Housing and Urban Development HUD. This program is specifically designed to help make credit available to borrowers who would otherwise not qualify for conventional loans on affordable terms. But, as the uniqueness of underground homes makes obtaining a mortgage more difficult, it also can make selling a home much harder.

Resale problems

Underground homes are more difficult to sell than conventional homes. For the consumer looking at new homes, an earth shelter provides an unfamiliar alternative. When marketed against other conventional houses, the underground home seller is at an unfair disadvantage.

The problem is similar to getting a mortgage on an atypical type of home. There currently exists very little data to validate the underground home design. The uneducated professional appraisers have trouble determining the value of them. For this reason, prospective home buyers are afraid of them. People unfamiliar with sheltered homes are unable to make a fair evaluation of them. Generally, consumers will be frightened by this. For the underground home seller, this fear of the unknown will translate into fewer market opportunities.

To sell underground homes, many resort to creative marketing. Rather than listing their homes with a regular real estate agent, they tend to be sold more by the owners. Another option is to list the earth-sheltered home with specialty real estate agents or one of the several websites that specialize in underground home listings. Again, the trick is having a real estate agent who is innovative and values this unique form of living. A real estate agent with knowledge of earth-sheltered homes can market the advantages more effectively, even though this can be a creative challenge. To many earth-sheltered homeowners, however, selling their home is not even considered a problem — they would never consider moving.

Water problems

Another disadvantage of underground homes lies with water infiltration problems. Though rare, this type of problem can be a much bigger complication than in a conventional home when it occurs below grade. With earth-sheltered homes, it is absolutely essential that water drainage systems be designed properly. They need to work the first time so you do not have to go back and fix them later; it is much less expensive to think ahead and design a proper waterproofing system than it is to go back a fix a major problem.

Improper site drainage, waterproofing, ventilation, and insulation are the biggest causes of water problems underground. Never underestimate this problem, as it can turn a wonderful home project into a huge headache. *Chapter 8 discusses how to properly waterproof an underground home.*

Energy balance problems

Underground homes are so energy efficient that sometimes the extreme efficiency can actually lead to problems. Improperly balancing energy inputs and outputs can lead to homes being too warm in the winter or too cold in the summer. This can also mean uncomfortable temperatures and dampness through condensation. Solving these problems involves a careful design of your home. Adequate ventilations and the correct balance of energy inputs and outputs to the home can keep this from being a concern later.

Pest, mold, and mildew problems

Properly constructed underground homes are safer from pests, mold, and mildew problems than their aboveground counterparts. Unfortunately, the reverse is also true if the home is not properly designed — these problems can be more abundant. The difficulties that can occur in any type of housing can be exaggerated by underground living. Because of the way underground homes are constructed, these sorts of problems can be harder to correct once they occur. Buried concrete forms 7 feet underground can lead to termite infestation, which is much harder to correct than it would be in the exterior wall of a conventional home. Mold problems that develop in an underground home are also harder to correct in a buried wall than they would be in an exposed, exterior wall. Earth-sheltered homes are usually much tighter homes than their conventional counterparts. Improper ventilation or insulation can lead to condensation problems, which can lead to mold and mildew. Unless you are building a mushroom factory, fungus growing in your home is not a desired outcome.

The improper use of materials can also lead to pest problems. Forms left buried on a poured wall can attract termites into a residence. Exterior wall penetrations that are not sealed properly allow burrowing rodents to infest a house. Generally pest, mold, and mildew problems are much more rare in underground homes. Proper design and construction will eliminate them entirely. *These important issues will be discussed in Chapter 3.*

Radon gas

Radon is an invisible, odorless, tasteless, and naturally radioactive gas. It is released in some areas of the country by the earth and products that contain natural earth materials. It is formed by the radioactive decay of naturally occurring radioactive elements found in earth. It is a hazard to all types of underground structures, including conventional basements because of their close contact with the earth. Radon gas is heavier than air and naturally accumulates in low areas of a home. The gas can seep through porous concrete from the earth or even diffuse out of shower water after the water has been pumped from an underground well. It can be a problem even in the most well-ventilated of homes.

Some areas of the country contain higher concentrations of radon gas than others, but elevated radon gas levels have been found in all states. The Environmental Protection Agency (EPA) maintains a map of what areas in the United States have high radon levels and what levels cause risks. This can be found at **www.epa.gov/radon/zonemap.html**.

It has been estimated that the average person received more exposure to radiation from radon gas than from all other natural or man-made radioactive sources combined. In underground homes, it is more of a matter of concern because of the increased ground contact. The danger from radon gas comes from long-term exposure to the natural radioactivity in the gas. *Ways to mediate this hazard from you home will be discussed in Chapter 9.*

Access problems

One final disadvantage earth-sheltered homes have is that it is harder to get into and out of them. Provisions for handicap access may be more difficult. Lot access may be harder to design, and emergency egress from a home may be harder to build to code. When you live totally underground it may even be more difficult for your friends to find you. Because the home is surrounded by dirt, some walls will remain inaccessible to doors and windows. Local building and fire codes for emergency access and egress must be met for a structure to be approved, which might seem like it would cause a problem for many earth-sheltered dwellings. Complete building codes vary by area, but you can usually get a complete copy of local building codes from your local building department. Some earth shelters solve this problem elegantly by creating two access doors to a room that might normally have one, or by adding an exit window on an interior wall. One interesting solution involved a roof exit door. These access problems must be addressed in the design phase of your home; otherwise, you might run into problems in the plan review.

The good news about underground homes is that even though there are some disadvantages, these can be easily overcome with proper design and a little bit of extra care in construction. Most of the problems are avoided by designing a home that has strong architectural appeal to both lenders and the market, which will make financing and marketing easier. The design should also include adequate provisions for waterproofing, insulation, and ventilation. It should include provisions for pest control, radon gas management, and building access per code. Proper design and planning are the keys to enjoying the benefits of earth shelters without any of the drawbacks.

Summary

Though living underground seems to offer some distinct advantages, it also has some disadvantages that need to be considered carefully before building your own earth-sheltered home. One important point is that as more people build earth-sheltered homes, the easier they will become to build for everyone. The permitting, financing, and even the resale value will become better. As energy becomes more and more expensive and people become more conscious of environmental conservation, the drive to build underground homes will become more pronounced. Ultimately, earth-sheltered homes may become much more popular than they are today. Because of the many benefits, many more people will consider them a more viable home building option. But, in order to fully understand the benefits earth-sheltered homes have to offer, you must understand how they were first created and built.

Chapter 2

The Oldest Abode: The History and Development of Earth-Sheltered Homes

"The charm of history and its enigmatic lesson consist in the fact that, from age to age, nothing changes and yet everything is completely different."
— *Aldous Huxley, English novelist*

Before You Build, Learn From The Past

It is important to consider the lessons of the history of earth-shelters before actually constructing one. The mistakes of the past can be avoided only by learning from it. Historical ideas from the construction of earth-sheltered homes can provide valuable insights for those who wish to build them in present times. Actually, the history of earth-sheltered homes is quite interesting. From the underground houses in Australia's abandoned Opal Mines to the cave homes in China, there are many fascinating structures from which to learn.

The history of earth shelter construction starts with the history of civilization itself. One does not have to look any farther than the pyramids to see excellent examples of civilizations using the earth as a construction material. With simple mud and straw, the ancient Egyptians built complex dormitory-like structures. Perhaps it was because wood was more valuable, but they learned the value of using earth as a building material early on. The advantages of using a material that was cheap, abundant, and easily workable were readily apparent. Every major civilization, from the Chinese dynasties in the Far East to the Celtic civilizations of Western Europe, developed some form of earth-shelter construction.

The full extent of how earth has been used for sheltering in different ways throughout history is a study too big for this book. Instead, the subject will be simplified by looking at a few interesting examples. To get a clear understanding, the three major types of earth-sheltered constructions will be discussed: in-hill, bermed, and in-ground construction. These three different types of constructions have been used throughout history as forms of shelter by one civilization or another, and all are still in use.

In-Hill Shelter Homes

The oldest type of earth-sheltered home is the in-hill shelter. The best example of this type of home is the cave, which has been an abode of mankind since the dawn of history. Most archeologists agree caves were the first human habitats. Constructed or excavated by groups of people living communally, they formed the first natural homes. It was not until construction techniques became more refined that mankind moved out of caves. They learned to build more complex homes of sod and wood, but earth was still a primary material for most of these structures. Even after this move, the benefits of cave living still remain; many people still reside in cave homes, as we shall see later in this chapter.

Native American homes

Our country has a rich history of in-hill sheltered living structures. The amazing architecture of the ancient Anasazi cliff dwellings shows that American Indian populations knew the value of using the earth as a shelter. These 700-year-old earth-sheltered homes are considered a historic treasure, and are worth visiting if you have the chance. Located at the base of Pikes Peak in Colorado, tours of the dwellings are open seven days a week, except on major holidays.

A quick tour of these dwellings is like taking a trip into the past. By examining these homes, one can see how these native people really lived. The structures contain rooms for grain storage, cooking, and sleeping. For these people, earth shelters had an additional interesting feature. Living in the side of a high cliff protected them from more aggressive tribes of people. Built on the side of a hill, steep access, ladders, ramps, and other defensive features were built into these cliff homes. The young were trained on where to find the safe handholds and how to pull ladders up at night. During times of enemy attack, these dwellings were thought to be almost impenetrable because there was no way to get into them. For this reason these tribes where able to develop more stable societies. Safe in their cool cliff shelters, the natives could live and sleep secure from any threat.

Another interesting collection of Native American dwellings are the Mesa Verde cliff dwellings, also found in Colorado. These native people originally lived in pit houses, another type of earth shelter that consisted of an excavated pit covered by poles, brush, and clay. In 1066, a volcanic eruption covered their territory with ash, perhaps one of the reasons the people migrated to the Verde Valley, where they constructed elaborate masonry cliff dwellings in the sides of the river bluff. Living there for close to 400 years, the natives developed a complex society that included trade, art, and developed family structures. Intense pressure on the land ultimately forced these early Americans to leave their homes in the 1400s. Spanish explorers found the homes completely abandoned roughly 200 years later. Evidence of their cultural advancement was left behind for all to see.

Mesa Verde Cliff Dwellings

*All photos of Mesa
Verde courtesy of
Trip McConkey*

The Gila Cliff dwellings in New Mexico are another excellent example of Native American earth-sheltered cave homes. Dug into the side of a volcanic cliff, the Mogollon people lived here as early as 1275 A.D. The caves provided deep shelters that where surrounded by woods that hid the openings. Occupied by up to 15 families at a time, these cave dwellings were also abandoned in the 1300s but are still an amazing testament to the way these people lived and developed.

The opal mine homes of Coober Pedy

Perhaps the most interesting twist on the in-hill shelters is the opal mine homes of Coober Pedy in South Australia. Known as the opal capital of the world, this sparsely populated area has many opal mines that were cut into the surrounding hillside and hard ground. When the mines were abandoned, some were converted into residences. Recent excavations have also created new cave homes. It turns out the cost of excavating a three-bedroom cave home with a living room, kitchen, and bathroom is about the same or less than what it takes to construct a conventional home in this area. One abandoned mine has even been converted to a Serbian Orthodox Church. This underground church, which serves as a tourist attraction in the town, draws in many visitors each year. This area is a desert with all extremes of weather in both the summer and winter. Cave dwellers in this small town have found it much more comfortable to live underground. Cut out of the hard ground, these cave homes are extremely cost-effective, as they require no additional materials for structural support. Many have all the comforts of a modern home. The only noticeable difference is that they have walls and ceilings made of dirt.

Cave Church at Coober Pedy

Coober Pedy church photos courtesy of Trip McConkey

Other cave dwellings

Though cave homes can still be found in some areas of the United States, they are not very common in recent times because of a cultural feeling that cave living is primitive and undesirable. Cave homes are, however, very common in other parts of the world. One of the most famous collections of cave homes is the Andalucian cave houses of Granada, Spain. Here, homes are carved out of sheer rock cliffs and fit with all the amenities of 21st century living. Some homes even boast hot tubs and broadband cable connections. The cave home has become a cultural way of living in this area.

Cave dwellings are also extremely popular in China, where it is estimated that more than 40 million people live in this type of home. Without the cultural aversion that Westerners have for living underground, these Chinese cave dwellings have become a matter of tradition and common sense. Today, many are equipped with refrigerators and some are even wired for cable TV. The caves themselves are called "Yaodong" and are carved out of yellow earth, which is easy to dig. These caves are found mostly in the vast loess plateau in Northern China. During World War II, many of these cave homes also served as protection from the invading Japanese armies. They are easy to construct and maintain, and they provide great shelter from the elements, which keep the inhabitants cool in the summer and warm in the winter. Many of these Chinese cave inhabitants are said to miss their homes when they are forced to move to other areas.

Photo Courtesy of David Darling.

Caves on Mars

Though in-hill shelter homes are interesting, they generally are not the typical type of earth-sheltered construction; at least, not in the United States. They are, however, the least expensive and most practical type to build. They offer all of the advantages of underground living, and the importance of this type of construction has not been lost to some future homebuilders. NASA has recently spent money studying how natural caves on the moon and Mars can be used in man's eventual colonization of space. Who knows — perhaps the most popular way of living on other planets in the future will involve a return to cave living.

Bermed Construction

Bermed construction consists of earth piled against the sidewalls of a structure in a mound. Here, earth is usually tapered down and away from the structure on the side exterior walls of the structure. Probably the most familiar earth-bermed homes are not really earth-bermed homes at all. These are similar to the hobbit houses in Tolkien's famous series of books on Middle Earth. Simply put, these earth domes are bermed and covered with earth, but most bermed homes just have their walls covered with earth.

Earth-berming has been used for many years as a common way to create storage in the Midwestern United States, as it is used to store potatoes and other perishable crops. Underground bunkers keep potatoes cool all winter and increase their shelf life. Bermed shelters are also the most common way that the military stores ammunition. Bermed military storage bunkers are extremely stable and safe from disaster.

The term "berm" actually comes from military jargon for the level space between two parapet walls. It was intended as a way to fortify a military structure and keep it stable even in the advent of an explosive collapse. One of the most interesting bermed fortifications sits in Halifax, Nova Scotia. Most of it survived the largest non-nuclear explosion when a ship filled with munitions in Halifax Harbor blew up during the Second World War

Earth bermed house photo courtesy of Earth Sheltered Technologies, Inc.

Earth-bermed construction often occurs above grade and involves the construction of a berm wall, which is later backfilled. Because it is above grade and easy to drain, this type of construction produces fewer water infiltration problems than other types of earth shelters. With no earth cover, it is also structurally easier to build. Many of the structural problems of an underground home are eliminated by removing the weight of an earth covering. Bermed construction is one the most popular types of construction for an earth-sheltered home.

Five-thousand-year-old Skara Brae

One of the oldest examples of an earth-bermed structure is the 5,000-year-old Skara Brae on Orkney Island off the coast of Scotland. This site is a collection of ten clustered houses that formed a Neolithic village. This ancient structure shows the best way to create a bermed home — a method that avoids the use of wood for a berm wall. Younger developments, which used wood beams to hold back earth, have all effectively decayed. Skara Brae used stone walls, however, to hold back the earth, and has remained intact as a standing village for more than 5,000 years. Even heavily treated lumber has a buried life of only five to eight years. Thus, wood is not a good material to use for holding back the earth.

Berm walls can be constructed of concrete, masonry, stone, metal, or other types or exotic materials. Backfilled with earth, they have almost all the advantages of underground construction, without the heavy structural loads of an earth cover. Maintenance costs may be a bit higher than with in-hill construction, but the benefits are about the same. With bermed structures, a little more heat energy is lost through the roof structure, but energy savings are still roughly 95 percent that of an in-hill or in-ground constructed shelter. Conventional homes are insulated to R-40, whereas earth-covered homes gets about R-1 per inch of earth, plus any applied insulation. Thus, the savings is not in the insulation but in the tempering effects of the earth.

There are many examples of modern earth-bermed architecture. This type of design is seen in schools, industrial parks, and office buildings. Architecturally, earth-berming reduces the footprint of the home and helps it blend into the landscape.

In-Ground Construction

The last type of earth shelter is called in-ground construction. This is considered by some to be a true underground house. It involves the excavation and construction of the whole structure slightly or completely below grade with an earth cover. Walls can be bermed or placed below ground level, and the roof structure is completely covered with 6 inches to 10 feet of earth. The value of an earth cover begins to decrease rapidly at more than 3 feet, so most covers are 3 feet or less. Because it involves more excavation, or movement of earth, this type of earth-sheltered construction is more expensive. Structural and water infiltration problems are also more common.

Bill Gates' mansion

One of the most famous in-ground homes built in modern times, lies on the shores of Lake Washington in Seattle. Completed at a cost of approximately $136 million. This house belongs to software mogul William (Bill) Gates III and his family. Set into the lake hillside, this residence, nicknamed Xanadu 2.0, looks much smaller than its 66,000 square feet would suggest. The home looks just like any other large Pacific Northwest home from the perspective of a boat on the lake, but the hidden areas underground are what make the difference. The house itself has 24 bathrooms, seven bedrooms, many living rooms, six kitchens, and six fireplaces. Having every amenity imaginable, the structure is perhaps the most amazing example of what can be done using modern materials and the earth. The home comes complete with a 2,000-square-foot domed library, a 92-foot-long grand staircase, a movie theater, a ten-car underground garage, and a commercial-grade kitchen. Designed to look like a typical Northwestern lodge home, the property hides a large gym, a 17 feet by 60 feet swim area with a built-in underwater sound system, and even a stream stocked with wild salmon.

As you can imagine, building a mansion of this sort takes some time to complete — seven years, to be exact. The amenities, however, were not the only things that made building and designing this house a lengthy task. Because of

Pictures courtesy of re-designday.com

its famous owner's background, the mansion was designed to incorporate all the latest technology. Guests are given a microchip badge that controls lighting and heating as they move from room to room. The floors are also said to be pressure sensitive so a security teams knows where you are at all times. A 22-foot computer display in the conference room is made up of 24 40-inch video display screens. While the main home was being constructed, Gates is said to have lived in the 1,900-square-foot underground guest house. Quite a dream home but also not an inexpensive way to live, especially when you consider the property taxes in 2009 were assessed at $1.063 million per year.

Buckminster Fuller's underground domes

One of the most interesting alternative building structures is the geodesic dome developed by scientist and inventor R. Buckminster Fuller. Because of its inherent shape, it is a natural design to develop for underground homes. This semi-spherical design requires few materials and is structurally strong. Geodesic domes were considered excellent candidates for underground housing. The domes have an extremely high strength-to-material ratio.

Some of the first underground domes tested their compressive strength by parking a Caterpillar D8 across the roof structure. When geodesic domes were first introduced during the 1950s, it was thought that many people would use this structure for home construction. But, only about 50,000 geodesic homes had been built by the 1980s, and even fewer have been used underground. Why this is so is usually attributed to the uniqueness of the dome structure and its unfamilarity with the general public. Whether or not it will become more popular in the future is hard to say.

Converted missile silo shelters

Another very interesting adaptation of the in-ground constructed underground home is seen in the many converted ICBM and Atlas missile silos. Originally even more expensive to build than the Gates' mansion, many of these abandoned relics of the Cold War have been converted into livable shelters. Consisting of collections of missile tubes, control bunkers, and huge blast doors, these strange structures have been modified into homes. Some even come with all the benefits of a true home: One recently converted silo auctioned off on eBay for $1.5 million, boasts a 1,100-gallon hot tub, a home theater, and 16,000-square-feet of finished living space. Other online sites offer missile silo condos and missile silo country homes. Hardened with hundreds of tons of reinforced steel and concrete, these silos were designed to survive an almost direct nuclear attack. A few of these homes are sold today as a safe way to survive an uncertain future and advertised as some of the most unique homes in existence. The silo home is not for everyone; left to deteriorate for more than 50 years, some are completely filled with water. One water-filled silo in Arlington, Texas is offered as a scuba diving site. Most of the silos were built in the 1960s, and the original purchase prices were as low as $150,000. Most sell in the millions and still require more money to clean up and make them livable.

CASE STUDY: LIVING IN AN UNDERGROUND MISSILE SILO

Ed & Dianna Peden
20th Century Castles, LLC
P.O. Box 4
Dover, KS 6420
www.missilebases.com
info@missilebases.com
(785) 256-6029

When I first contacted Ed and Dianna Peden at 20th Century Castles, LLC, I was very surprised by their response. Their e-mail outlined the features of their underground missile silo home like this:

"My wife and I have lived 15+ years in a decommissioned harden underground missile silo structure. We have over 18,000 square feet of underground space. Of this about 6,500 square feet we consider our home and the rest is garage and shop space. A 120-foot tunnel connects the two structures. Our garage door is 47 tons and this keeps the shop quite secure. The temperature in our home is easily managed and quite comfortable. Seasonal variations are minimal this deep in the ground. Humidity is more of a challenge than heat control. The home has a large greenhouse sun room that brings natural light into the home. We burn wood heat in the winter months. An interest

in earth-contact housing in the 1970s got us interested in this type of unique property. Our full earth-over structure is very well built and will last for centuries. We never fear Kansas tornadoes."

After reading their correspondence, I realized their living situation is not as unique as I first thought. According to the Peden's, they have closed more than 50 sales of this type of unique property over the last 15 years. Their website currently includes listing for more than 12 government sites from Lewis, NY to Medical Lake, Wash. The properties have prices anywhere from $199,000 for a Nike missile site in Gardner. Kan. to more than $2 million for an Atlas F missile site with a private FAA approved runway. I found the information including tour videos of some of the bunkers fascinating. This certainly is a unique way to live.

Safe structures

In-ground structures are very popular, but they have limitations. These often relate to the structural requirement necessary to hold an earth cover. The structure required to carry an earth load of thousands of pounds of dirt must be much stronger than a structure in a conventional home. For the military with millions of dollars to spend, designing such homes is not a problem, but for the average homeowner, it can be expensive. The deeper the cover, the more expensive it becomes. This is why most earth covers are limited to from 6 to 8 inches.

Severe creaking noises occurred on the roof backfill of a local builder's project near Boulder, Colorado, causing him to double-check his engineer's structural calculations. A small error was found in the weight of the dirt being applied to the structure that could have spelled disaster if the builder had not been more alert.

Several collapsed underground structures have also raised concern about this type of earth-sheltered home. Though extremely rare, these problems have given in-ground structures a bad reputation that is undeserved. Most structural problems occur in non-engineered and experimental structures. These are structures that are not reviewed and stamped by a structural engineer. Structural failures in engineered structures are extremely rare.

One collapse of an engineered underground parking garage at Seward Park Houses in New York in 1999 occurred after very heavy rains. A review of the structure's design suggested engineering weaknesses in the calculation of the water weight of the soil might have been related to the collapse. Most engineers agree it is important to consider all live and dead loads to a structure. Dead loads are the structural loads of the weight of the structure and things that remain constant over the life of the structure. Live loads include the weight of things added. As it turns out, dirt loads are just part of the problem. In order to properly engineer a structure, you must include every weight that can be carried by a structure. This includes water, snow, wind, and any other loads that might be applied to the structure.

For example, the Amundsen-Scott South Pole Station was built underground in 1956 to protect its inhabitants from severe weather in Antarctica. This station had to be abandoned in 1975 because heavy snow accumulations eventually led to the collapse of the wooden structure that held it up. The snow loads at the South Pole were never fully appreciated when this structure was designed.

Structural troubles can be a problem on any type of construction. Most structural failures in underground buildings seem to be related to poor design or planning, but it is always wise to err on the side of caution. If you are building an in-ground style home, be sure to check the following things:

1. Your engineering is done properly.
2. Any concrete is cured properly.
3. The placement of dirt over the roof structure is done correctly.
4. Any additional loads that may be added must be carefully considered. This includes snow loads, landscaping, and parking loads, if applicable.

If you are planning to park on top of the structure, make sure you plan for this.

Current Developments

Most modern, earth-sheltered homes are designed structurally and architecturally to be ideally suited to the building site, climate conditions, and tastes of the owner. Architects learning from the past have included provisions in the design of underground structure to ensure stability, longevity, water protection, and aesthetic appeal.

One of the biggest, more recent ideas is to take advantage of the sun to heat your home and make it more comfortable. This is something that was not fully understood by past builders of underground homes. New building science has perfected the art of using thermal mass, southern exposure, and passive solar heating to heat underground housing efficiently and reliably.

Another big development in underground homebuilding science has come with an understanding of how to protect homes from water infiltration, and how to properly ventilate and insulate a home. *Some of these new developments will be discussed in Chapter 8.*

CASE STUDY: MAKING GOOD DESIGN CHOICES FOR EARTH-SHELTERED HOMES

Kelly Hart, Earth-shelter Architect
GreenHomeBuilding.com
P.O. Box 632
Crestone,CO 81131
www.greenhomebuilding.com
Kellyhart@greenhomebuilding.com
(719) 588-3688
(866) 392-5743 (fax)

Designing an earth-sheltered home is much different than designing a conventional home. Some of the biggest differences are the choices available to the underground homebuilder. In America, we are culturally conditioned to believe that earth shelters are not the kind of places people should live. The culture supports a view that these types of homes are dark, dank, and dirty places to live, but this cannot be further from the truth. My experience has shown that earth-sheltered homes can be comfortable, sustainable, and wonderful places to live. They can be more energy efficient, aesthetically appealing, and sustainable than any other type of home. It is all about the design choices we make.

The initial choice of using earth shelters offers many more advantages than disadvantages. The biggest advantages of an earth-sheltered home are the energy benefits it offers. These energy savings can be further enhanced by using southern exposure and passive solar heating. Large thermal masses can be incorporated into a structure to collect and hold heat, then radiate it back slowly to the structure. The efficiency of wood heating is also greatly enhanced in earth shelters.

A secondary advantage of using the earth as a building material is that the natural footprint on your property is greatly reduced. Instead of creating an angular eyesore to the property, bermed or earth-covered homes can be designed to blend right into the natural harmony of the landscape. They can take advantage of the natural features of a property to add a comfortable feel that conventional construction sometimes misses. The structure can become a cozy and snug part of your living environment.

A third advantage involves the many new materials that are available for earth-sheltered construction. I am partial to the use of natural stone and materials that are native to an area. The use of natural materials makes the home warmer and helps it blend even better into the natural landscape.

Over the past few years, many new types of materials have been developed for use in earth-sheltered homes. Some of these are appealing because they are extremely sustainable. I have experimented with earth-bagged construction and papercrete finishes. Both of these use natural materials that can save significant money and resources.

Earth bagging is an extremely sustainable building material because you are actually using the earth itself to build your structure. Using a recycled-paper fiber stucco called papercrete is another way to create durable and attractive finishes. The use of earthship materials or used automobile tires, is also an extremely sustainable idea. This building philosophy has shown its value both for its sustainability and its economy. The use of used tires or salvaged cans offers a solution to a big environmental headache. You can learn more about my project at: **www. greenhomebuilding.com/earthbag.htm#ourhouse.**

The wide variety of choices in design makes earth-sheltered homes a wonderful alternative. Do not let the cultural biases influence your design decisions. Carefully consider the benefits an underground home can offer. These are homes that can help you save you energy. They are comfortable, appealing, and sustainable. Make good choices when you design your home.

Summary

It has been said that those who "refuse to learn from history are doomed to repeat it." What we can learn from the history of earth-sheltered homes has great practical value today. These structures are very long-lasting. We have learned that there are many different ways to use the earth for a home structure. Whether living in a cave, a bermed home, or completely underground (as in a missile silo), the earth has always been used, and is still being used today, as an effective housing structure. Whether it is being used as a home for the world's richest man or a common Chinese peasant, the earth can provide a comfortable lifestyle for all.

Chapter 3

The Best Laid Plans: Design, Planning, and Preparation to Build an Earth-Sheltered Home

"It pays to plan ahead. It wasn't raining when Noah built the ark."
— *Anonymous*

Even the best laid plans can still run into problems, but there is no substitute for good preparation. Good planning will make any construction project go more smoothly. It will also help make the project more affordable. In the following chapter, you will learn about some of the most important elements of planning an earth-sheltered home, from design considerations and where to get designs to how to site the designs to your property. Additionally, you will learn everything you need to know about what makes an earth-sheltered home different from a more conventionally designed home, why these differences are important, and how you can predict and control construction costs for an earth-sheltered home. For those of you getting ready to build an underground project, planning is the most important element. As Benjamin Franklin so wisely said, "An ounce of prevention is worth a pound of cure."

Earth Shelter Designs

Finding good house plans is the first step in any homebuilding process. Fortunately, there are many sources of quality underground house plans, which can be found online, through mail order, or in any major bookstore. The bad news, however, is that some of these plans may not work well with an underground home, but most can be adapted.

Starting from scratch

Do-it-yourself homebuilders are often tempted to start by designing their own set of plans. Though this can be successfully done, there are some hazards. Home designs are more than just deciding where the rooms are going to go on a piece of paper. In order for a home design to work, the buildable elements must work; the home plan must be buildable. Homebuilders trying to build from a design that is not buildable will often run into problems deep into the construction process. They will find themselves having to make last minute, ad hock changes to the design because one of the elements is not working. If this is overlooked, it can degrade the quality of the building and lead to bigger problems later on. It is best to avoid these unplanned changes as much as possible. The best way to do this is to get amateur designed plans reviewed by a good homebuilder, designer, or architect. With underground plans, this also means finding someone familiar with this type of construction and paying him or her for help.

Designers

Another option most homebuilders use for plans is a home designer. Home designers are people who work specifically to draw up home plans. Generally, designers cost about one-half to one-third the cost of a full-blown architect. Their qualifications usually include years of experience drafting and designing home plans. This is an economical and practical way to get your house plans designed. Remember, you still need to find someone with earth-sheltered design experience to make sure you get a buildable plan.

Adapting a Plan

As mentioned earlier, many plans for earth-sheltered homes already exist. Some of these can be adapted to work for your purposes and still be buildable plans. Rooms can be changed around, amenities can be added, and the structural elements will stay the same. This is a good way to come up with an inexpensive workable set of plans. Generally, stock plans show how the structure is built and may provide a list of materials needed to construct the home. Room sizes and locations can be changed around, but you may want to have a structural review to make sure things work after you are done changing things. Changing the location of plumbing, electrical, and heating fixtures can cause the most problems.

Architects

The final source for house plans is perhaps one of the best — a good architect. Architects are more expensive than designers or stock house plans, but a good one is well worth the money, especially if you are designing a more difficult or customized home. Some architects even specialize in the design of underground homes. Finding a good architect is more art than science. Look for one that has done designs that appeal strongly to you. Interview any potential architect carefully about what he or she has done — you can even ask for references. In the end, the best architect is one you can trust and work with easily. The best are the ones who come up with continuously good ideas that you can appreciate. Good custom architect fees can run from 3 to 15 percent of a project's costs. Architect fees on a $300,000 dollar home would be from $9,000 to $45,000 using this formula.

A good architect can lead you through every step of the building process, helping you visualize what your home will look like when it is completed. Some even have three-dimensional, computerized design tools that allow you to do a virtual walkthrough of your new home before it is ever built. They can even help you select finishes and amenities for your new home. In the long run, money spent on a good architect can improve the livability of a house, which is essentially an investment for you, the owner or builder. Keep in mind that just because you can build a home does not mean you can live in it.

When you have a plan for your home, one additional beneficial step is to create a three-dimensional (3-D) model. This can be created out of cardboard or plastic foam. If you are using a designer or architect, he or she can help you build a simple model. If you are doing it yourself, there are many sources for learning how to build a 3-D home model. The model will help you visualize all of the elements of your home in three dimensions, something you may not be able to do if you are just looking at a blueprint. Simple home models can be made for several hundred dollars.

The most important thing about home plans, however, is to find a set that suits you. They should be functional, practical, and aesthetically pleasing to you because, after all, you are the one who will be living in it.

Economical plans

The plans you pick will have a huge impact on the money you spend for your house. To be as economical as possible, steer clear of complex designs that have more space than you need. The two factors that influence home cost the most are the complexity of the design and the size of the structure.

Whether you are doing the work yourself or having the work contracted, complex designs add labor and materials and are, consequently, more expensive. When trying to save money, the rule is to keep it simple.

The second way to keep your costs down is by designing your home to a reasonable size. The larger your house, the more materials you will need to build it. Because housing costs are usually figured by the square foot, the more square footage there is, the greater the expense. Try to dimension your house at an early stage for the most appropriate size for you and your family (or future family). Remember, earth-sheltered homes are harder to remodel than conventional homes, so plan accordingly.

Design Considerations

Underground homes are uniquely different from conventional homes. Your plans need to express this difference. Try to plan for these differences at the earliest part of your design process. Design the house so that it takes full advantage of your lot and all the best features, considering the differences. Take a quick look at some of these differences.

Assuring natural light

Conventional homes have natural light coming in from all sides, but earth shelters have some walls covered with earth. This blocks the natural sunlight that would normally come in the house from these windows, meaning natural sources of light need to be maximized in other ways. One way is to use southern exposure, which will help get the best natural light infiltration in both winter and summer months. In the northern hemisphere, the sun is always more exposed from the south. All homes with an unobstructed, or unblocked, view to the south get more sun. If your lot precludes a southern exposure, design the house to sit on the site with maximum light exposure. The Gates' mansion, for example, has a western exposure over Lake Washington. The western exposure over the lake gives him the most sunlight.

Another way to get more natural light uses atriums with interior courtyards. These are open areas in the center of a structure that allow light to come in from all directions. The atriums can be open or covered by glass, but they are usually situated in the center of the home, allowing light to penetrate from every direction. Besides providing additional natural light, atrium courtyards can provide a nice private outside living area shielded from the wind and outside

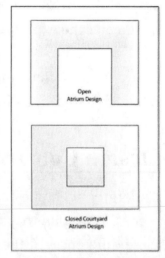

distractions. This private little courtyard can only be viewed from the rooms that surround it, and therefore allow for an almost universal appeal in earth shelters. If your design does not allow for a four-sided atrium, consider a three-sided, U-shaped one. Design the homes so that the U-shape faces the best light exposure.

Other design features that help add light are the use of skylights and light tubes. Most people are familiar with skylights, which are simple roof windows. Most skylights in conventional homes are used to let additional light in from the roof. These roof windows can be used in underground homes with the same result. Because access to the roof of your underground house may be easier, be sure to use protective glass, and be careful to protect people from falling through them.

Light tubes are less well known, but they also are great way to add extra light. In their simplest form, they consist of reflective tubes that allow outside light to travel greater distances into the structure. Acting as light periscopes, they allow light to penetrate deeper into your home. Light tubes can sometimes allow light into areas that would be inaccessible to a regular skylight. Known by many trade names, light tubes, sun scopes, sun pipes, or solar light pipes are reflective tubes that can be purchased at most building hardware stores, and are even something the novice builder can install. Although they are commonly used in modern-day building, the idea of collecting light from the outside and leading it into the structure is actually quite old. It was developed by the ancient Egyptians and has been rediscovered recently with the use of more modern materials.

Window Walls

Another way to increase light penetration is with the use of window walls, which is a wall made almost entirely of glass. Some really interesting designs include a window wall with a slightly angled window roof attached

Window wall photo courtesy of Robert McConkey

on the south or exposed side of the house. This acts as a sort of greenhouse attached to the exposed side of the home. A window wall can collect light even when the sun is high in the sky and is an excellent way to gather solar heat. Window walls can vary in cost, but the extra expense is usually well worth it.

Interior lighting

To make up for lost exterior light, many underground homeowners supplement their home lighting by increasing the interior lighting. The caves of Andalucia, Spain, and the Coober Pedy opal mine homes all have brightly lit interiors. Full spectrum light bulbs can allow for simulated sunlight to be in every room.

Conforming to building codes

Another important consideration in underground structural design is conforming to local building codes. If your plans do not meet the requirements of these codes, they will not be approved for construction. Most issues are fairly simple to address and will be caught in plan review. One issue that is a common problem is providing for proper egress, or exits, from the building in case of an emergency. Many building codes require that a structure have enough doors and windows to properly escape a fire or emergency. These escapes must be situated in every room. The standard form of escape can be an additional door or window. The constraints of being underground with earth-covered walls sometimes interferes with the ability to provide exits from every room. The way to get around these restrictions is to design two doors in a room or add an extra interior window. This might mean that a bathroom might have two entrance doors or a bedroom might have a window on an interior wall. The placement of these access points is important to your design. An architect or building designer should be able to help you with these types of problems. If you are not sure, you can always have your plans checked by the local building code official.

Providing for good drainage

Adequate drainage around your house is the single most important feature of an underground home design — good drainage and waterproofing are essential. Homes that sit above the ground do not need to worry about ground water, but underground homes are a sinking ship if water problems are not well planned for.

Make sure you are happy with your plan's design for waterproofing and feel it is adequate to handle any water infiltration, no matter how severe. An architect or soil engineer may be able to help you with this, but if you have any questions, make sure that you consult with an expert. Reducing the possibility of water problems in the future is well worth the effort.

Construction Materials

Other important and practical considerations for your home design are the types of materials and construction methods you will use. If you are working with an architect, he or she can help you with many of these decisions, but, either way, this is a good time to look at the options available.

Concrete construction

In modern home construction, one of the most commonly used and practical materials is reinforced concrete. Formed from a combination of cement, sand, stones, and water, this material has an almost universal appeal in underground construction. Reinforced concrete is durable, strong, and does not rot or decay when exposed to damp earth. Its durability is made evident by the ancient Roman roads and aqueducts that were built thousands of years ago and are still in use. Pozzolanic cement used in Roman aqueducts and roads will harden virtually forever.

Concrete can be cast in virtually any shape, and it is used in conventional construction for footing, foundations, and slab floors. This versatile material has many additional uses in underground structures. Concrete can be used for structural walls, beams, and roofing structures. It can be poured in place, or you can use precast panels. Precast concrete has been cast and cured at a factory and shipped to your construction site in a form ready to build with. This type of concrete offers higher quality and, in some cases, lower costs than casting your own concrete. The chief disadvantage in any type of concrete work is that it is not always the least expensive option. Complex designs require complex casting skills. These are skills that are developed over many years and are not to be attempted lightly.

Shotcrete

Shotcrete concrete is actually a common way to place concrete using a high-pressure hose instead of creating castings in a form. Most people are familiar with shotcrete or gunite concrete because this is how swimming pools are built. Shotcrete, concrete, and in some cases, mortar, which is concrete without the gravel, is shot out of the end. The product shot can be either wet or dry. When it is dry, it is often referred to as gunite. The compaction of the concrete is created by the force of the projected blast. Reinforcement is usually provided by steel reinforcing that forms the shape of the shell.

Shotcrete was actually invented by a taxidermist in the early 1900s as a way to fill plaster models of animals. Since then, it has developed into a patching method to repair the weak parts of damaged buildings. Recently, shotcrete has been used for everything from pools to concrete floating docks. The technology has be developed so that thin-shelled shotcrete can be used in home construction, retaining walls, and even floating ships.

Though shotcreting takes some skill, some companies specialize in providing pre-fabricated shotcrete superstructure shells that can be easily erected to form the walls and ceiling of an underground home. These shells can be manufactured in one part of the country and shipped almost anywhere for erection.

CASE STUDY: PRECAST
CONCRETE PANELS

Dale Pearcey Founder & President
Formworks Building, Inc.
P.O. Box 1509
Durango, CO 81302
formworks@rmi.net
www.formworksbuilding.com
(907) 247-2100
(970) 247-9190 (fax)

It was the oil crisis of 1970 that was the catalyst for Formworks Building, Inc., to begin exploring the earth-shelter market. During this time sustainable and affordable housing demanded innovation and thinking differently about home construction. Dale Pearcey, founder and president of Formworks Building, Inc., had served on the American Concrete Institute's committee of Shotcreting for thin shell construction and had been a certified energy rater for the state of Colorado. His company had won many awards and citations for their work, including a citation by the Colorado governor and an award for energy innovation by the U.S. Department of Energy.

Pearcey actually lived in the first home the company built in 1979 and since then the company has helped construct more than 2,000 structures across the United States and Canada. Pearcey still lives and works in an earth sheltered home and says he often takes for granted the comfort and security it provides his family. The biggest comfort to him is his energy bills, which are consistently 10 percent of his neighbors.

He believes the reason more people do not live in these types of homes is a lack of knowledge about how they work. As the self-proclaimed largest earth-shelter builder in the world, it is his mission to help educate people. While doing this, he has set a standard of excellence for his company in the industry.

Formworks has developed their own precast building system that is so flexible, it can be used to create "virtually any space the customer can imagine." Unlike other systems which create small pods that link together, Formwork's system offers cathedral ceilings with large, unobstructed clear spans. The system is designed to be erected by anyone and can be shipped anywhere in the world. Detailed parts lists and assembly instructions allow an owner/builder to erect the system using unskilled labor.

According to Pearcey, permitting has never been a problem with Formworks system. With their system, interior framing, plumbing, and electrical are done similarly to a conventional home. All of their shell components are structurally engineered by a registered engineer and meet state building codes. Formworks was even the first designer in the country to achieve a fully financed conventional home loan for an earth shelter through the FHA program.

Formworks patented steel-reinforced concrete shell system is very innovative. It uses thin shell shotcrete, a form of reinforced concrete that is actually sprayed on in thin layers. The lighter structure is designed to be economical, structurally strong, and durable. The system even comes with a special water-proofing system designed by the company. Because the system is so user friendly, costs are quite reasonable. Formworks homes have been rated by the FHA with a life of 85 years, as opposed to conventional homes, which carry a 30 year rating. Pearcey thinks because concrete is covered by earth the life span of these structures may be in the hundreds of years.

The Formworks company has worked very hard to develop a building system that works well with earth-sheltering. When most people object to underground homes because light cannot penetrate the ground, Pearcey flatly counters that it cannot penetrate a roof, either. One of the most interesting stories he tells is when his great grandmother toured his newly completed home shortly after it had been built. As the tour was coming to a close, she politely turned to him and asked, "Well, when do we get to the underground part?"

Several customer Web sites are available to view Formwork's product, one is a YouTube video, at **www.youtube.com/watch?v=hhkr-e5Jk_k&feature=autofb**, and the other is a client's home website, at **www.dragonflyhill.org**.

Pearcey said the only pest problem he has with his earth-sheltered home is the pizza boy who bugs him to tour the inside of his home. He loves him, but thinks the best solution to the problem might be to go on a diet. To Pearcey, earth-sheltered homes offer too many advantages to consider living anywhere else. He figures the energy savings alone will allow a homeowner to pay a mortgage off in 15 years, rather than 30 years, and after that the homes and energy savings are theirs to enjoy for a long time.

Although it is a popular building item for underground homes, a practical disadvantage to concrete is that it is not waterproof in its natural form. This is something many people discover for the first time when their slightly porous concrete basement starts leaking very slowly. I learned this in the concrete float business, when we used to cast concrete floating docks. The original concrete floats were cast around a paraffin-coated cardboard box. The problem was that the concrete covers would leak over time, causing the float to eventually sink — not a good outcome for a dock. To alleviate this problem, the new float designs have a polystyrene core that absorbs very little water and keeps the dock floating.

The good news is that concrete can be kept from leaking with additives that can be attached to the surface of the concrete to make it impenetrable to water. *Many of these ideas will be discussed in the waterproofing section of this book.*

Concrete is the preeminent building material in underground construction. It can be made as hard as rock by varying the amount of cement, with strengths in excess of 7,000 pounds per square inch (PSI). Although not as cheap as other types of building materials, concrete will virtually last forever.

The foundation of your underground home is not the only part of the building phase where you may wish to use concrete, though. The cement in concrete can also be used in many types of finishes. Stucco, papercrete, and epoxy cement can be used as finished exterior coatings on exposed walls instead of wood siding. Cement and sand mortars can also be used as binding agents in masonry construction.

Masonry Construction

Second only to concrete, masonry can be used for wall construction and structural support. Reinforced masonry block, brick, or stone offers a durable and more attractive alternative to concrete. Natural stone or adobe brick can be used to accent the natural harmony of the structure. Many different stone options exist, from round river rock to imported marble or slate. Naturally occurring stone collected near the area in which you are building can also be used economically. Masonry block and bricks also come in a wide range of options: broken-faced, fluted, exposed aggregate, and textured block. Visiting a masonry block shop and viewing the different styles can help you appreciate the wide range of options.

Masonry's chief disadvantage as a building material, however, is that it is very labor-intensive. Paying a mason to erect a block wall can be very expensive. Owner labor can make it less expensive, but there is a steep learning curve required in learning how to doing it right.

Another recently added construction technology is the use of dry stack masonry block. Here, concrete blocks are stacked without the use of any mortar. Gravity holds the blocks in place until they can be secured later. The blocks are held in place permanently with reinforced-concrete poured columns. This has the advantage of saving expensive mason labor because the blocks only need to be stacked, not mortared together. The interior hollow spaces in the blocks are later filled with reinforced concrete. The blocks act as a form for the concrete columns that never have to be stripped. Although this makes building less expensive, the biggest disadvantage to dry stack blocks is that the finished appearance is not always as nice as a masonry block wall. The joints can be uneven and blocks can easily get out of alignment.

Steel construction

The use of steel as a construction material has recently had a major resurgence in residential construction. High lumber costs in the 1980s made using steel studs, steel "I" beams, and posts more common as structural components in all types of housing. As lumber gets more expensive, steel will probably become more attractive, especially because it has the advantage of being extremely durable, recyclable, and can be engineered more easily then wood.

Creative uses of half culverts and steel Quonset huts have been incorporated into underground structures with great success, allowing for a unique home design. The arched steel is can be placed in the side of a hill, bermed, or buried. One of the most interesting storage structures I have seen was a steel storage shipping container that was bermed and covered with dirt. This used extremely inexpensive steel shipping containers that must be engineered for a dirt cover. One creative architect even designed a buried steel storage container that was waterproofed and used as a swimming pool.

Though steel allows for creative uses and design, it can be expensive. Also, keep in mind that unprotected steel that comes in contact with water will rust, so waterproofing is important. Be careful with anything you design using steel, as grades of steel can vary. Also, make sure anything that is structural is well-engineered. It is important to use only properly designed steel materials in your structure. One corrugated steel culvert company became upset when they learned that their piping was being cut in half and used as a part of a living structure. Their lawyer's response stated strongly that their pipe was only to be used in its original round configuration, and was not engineered to be used for underground living. Improper use of this steel piping that was specifically designed to carry water might collapse if used as the structural support of a home.

Post and beam construction

Post and beam construction has been used successfully in earth-sheltered construction, primarily as structural supports. It is important that wood is protected from direct exposure to the soil. Post and beam construction is specialized enough that anyone interested in building with it should research this type of building system specifically. Any post and beam construction must be engineered specifically for the structural loads of soil, snow, and other anticipated live loads. Improperly engineered structures cannot only lead to collapse, but also to cracks and other defects in the home structure.

Conventional wood framing

Regardless of what materials you use to build your underground house, conventional wood framing will probably be a part of it. Wood studs are the best choice for exterior-exposed walls and interior partition walls. Wood floor joist and plywood or car decking is still the best for second-floor framing. Likewise, wood posts and glulam beams are still good choices for structural support posts. Glulam, or glue-laminated, beams are composite wood beams made from smaller wood pieces glued together to make structural beams. They are usually a much less expensive alternative than using large natural wood beams. The use of natural woods inside your residence can accent the use of the earth outside. Traditional wood siding can also be used on any unburied exterior walls.

Alternate Construction Materials

Probably some of the most exciting new building materials are ones that the conventional builder is unfamiliar with. Most of these have come to be used only in the last few decades. The advantage of these new materials is that many of them are inexpensive and easy to erect. Because they are new, many of these building materials still present challenges. If you are planning on incorporating any of them in your home, make sure to research them carefully. Using new materials can be rewarding, but it can also be a huge frustration for the new builder. If you are adventurous, they offer some exciting alternatives, but if you are more cautious, use them with care.

Earth bagging

Imagine building a durable home structure out of the dirt on your property. One new building material promises this: earth bagging. Similar to a free-formed, rammed earth building style, earth bagging involves the use of plastic bags filled with dried

Photo courtesy of ***www.tinyhousedesign.com***

dirt. Pioneered by architect Nader Khalili at the California Institute of Earth Art and Architecture, earth bags are similar to sand bags, but much harder. The bags can be stacked and arched to create the super structure of a house. Woven polypropylene plastic bags are filled with a mixture of earth and water and allowed to dry until they become rock hard. The bags provide a formed structure to the earth inside. These bags are then stacked to create a structural wall. Wire mesh or barbed wire is used between the bags for reinforcing. Proper stacking of these bags can lead to self-supporting arched doors and windows.

Corbelled bags can be use to create a domed roof structure. Corbelling involves offsetting each bag just a little to create an arch (this building material is ideally suited to small circular domed structures). The main advantage of earth in a bag is that it is extremely inexpensive. For the price of a few bags, some wire reinforcing, and free earth, anyone can stack up a structural wall in a few days. Plus, the use of earth bags can eliminate more than 95 percent of the wood used in a structure.

If you choose to build with this material, remember that it is still somewhat experimental. Earth-bagged structures are harder to engineer and not always readily acceptable by local building officials. The International Conference of Building Officials, ICBO, tests these products for use in all home building applications, and testing is still being done. Some building codes will not accept non-ICBO-tested materials. Also, some types of soils do not bond well to themselves; because of this, some soils cannot be used to make good earth bags.

Sandbags have been used for many years to provide protection from flooding and in military fortifications, but these structures are usually temporary. Earth bags are designed to provide permanent wall structures that can be plastered over with a finished surface. Earth bags may sound like a foreign idea, but it is estimated that more than one-quarter of the world's population lives in earth-formed shelters of some kind. Earth bags are a very simple way to form the earth and use it for shelter, although they are not always used as earth-formed shelters. The technology may even be used to improve upon third world earth-sheltered housing. To learn more about earth bagging, visit **www.motherearthnews. com/Green-Homes/2005-10-01/Earthbag-Construction.aspx**.

Cordwood construction

Another interesting building material is something called cordwood masonry. This used to be referred to as stackwood construction. Here, round logs cut to the thickness of a wall are held together like a stack of cordwood in a mortar binder. This building methodology has

Cordwoood home Photo courtesy **www.motherearthnews.com**

been shown to have many advantages over conventional construction. Cordwood walls are inexpensive, easy to erect, and energy-efficient. Cut rounds of cordwood are stacked and mortared together, much like block or stone. The mortaring takes less skill than regular masonry mortaring and provides a finished result that is aesthetically pleasing. What is visible is the round end cuts of wood set in a mortar bed. This view shows all the natural round growth rings of the tree, adding a natural appeal to the structure. Scrap wood that is unsuitable for making lumber can be used, saving you money and resources. The thick cordwood that makes up about 50 percent of the wall structure also provides a good thermal mass. This type of material is thought to combine the advantages of a wood wall with the aesthetics of a wall of masonry.

Again, cordwood construction is fairly new, so any disadvantages may not yet be well known. The cordwood in contact with any earth must be protected, which poses the question of how long the cordwood will hold up. If it is kept dry, the cordwood will probably hold up for a long time, but no one knows for sure. One interesting variation I saw on cordwood construction is the use of recycled glass bottles instead of wood as the wall material. If you want to learn more about cordwood construction, visit the Earthwood Building School at **www.cordwoodmasonry.com/ Cordwood.html**.

Earthship construction

*Earthship photo courtesy of **www.earthship.org***

Another recent, alternative building method is Earthship. As more of a philosophy than an actual building material, it tries to combine the best of ideas about building sustainable, recycled structures. These structures are designed to be "living building systems" that address every human need. The crux of Earthship construction is using materials that are green, or eco-friendly.

*Window Wall in Earthship photo courtesy of **www.earthship.org***

Most Earthship structures have passive solar heating and use the earth and recycled materials for a thermal mass. Walls are usually built of hard-to-recycle products, such as automobile tires or aluminum and steel cans, filled with rammed earth. This material is inexpensive and extremely durable, as items like the tires are said to have a lifespan of dozens of centuries. Building with these materials also allows you to help recycle things that would otherwise not be used.

The whole philosophy of Earthship design is living in natural harmony with the environment, recycling materials, and living sustainably. Because of this, these homes usually have natural adobe covers and allow for low power and energy consumption, along with the recycling of septic and water systems.

In addition to offering many of the advantages of earth bagging, Earthship building also makes good sense. Resources on Earth are limited, and builders are helping preserve Earth by helping recycle and sustain these resources. The technologies are still relatively new, but the appeal is strong. Building with items like used tires has actually created local shortages of used tires in some areas of the country.

One chief concern with used tires is that toxic gasses may be released by old tires. This is what gives them that rubbery smell, but out-gassing, or the release of gasses, by rubber tires has been extensively tested and has not been found to be a problem. One main benefit in the use of tires is the significant reduction in the use of lumber. Earthship homes can use 90 percent less lumber, notably saving forest resources. Because of the many advantages to this type of building, you may hear more about Earthship homes in the future. If you wish to learn more, visit **www.earth-ship.net/buildings.html**.

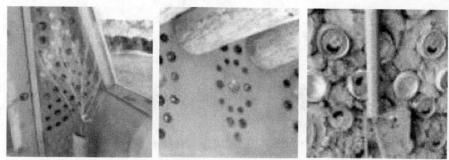

*Bottles and cans in wall photo courtesy of **www.earthship.org**.*

One interesting area in Earthship building is called carbon zero building. Here, energy consumption and the environmental use of building resources is reduced to minimal levels. This idea is an area that is supported by Earthship biotexture at **www.earth-ship.org**. Proponents of green buildings are fighting the long waits for permits necessitated by such extremely new methods of construction like Earthship by looking for what they call pockets of freedom. These freedom areas, such as Eastern Montana, do not require any building permits at all and allow experimental Earthship homes to be built immediately. Other areas like di-saster relief building in Haiti also allow economical zero carbon structures to be built. The hope here is that by building more of these structures people will become more familiar with how they work and their advantages.

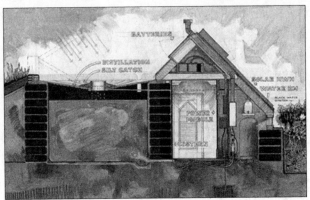

*Photo courtesy of **www.earthship.org***

At the writing of this book, the state of Florida was getting its first Earthship home — a home billed as a sustainable and self-supporting structure. It is constructed entirely of recycled materials and earth. The builder has collected many recycled bottles and cans but is asking the community through its website (**www. earthshipfloridaproject.com**) for 20,000 more. The house gets its water from collecting rainwater and it recycles the water four times. Toilets are flushed with non-smelling grey water from the sinks and shower. The septic waste water is used to grow food. Water is heated with natural gas and the sun and electricity is generated with wind and solar power.

Other materials

Many alternate building materials can also be used in underground houses. None are discussed in detail in this book, but they are worth mentioning. Earth-sheltered homes have been constructed of adobe bricks, rammed earth, hay bales, straw and mud, cob, hemp, bamboo, wattle and daub, and clay. Some of these alternative building materials are gaining popularity, as rammed earth and straw bale homes have been built in every area of the country. The use of natural materials can offer strength, economy, natural insulation, and aesthetic advantages. Organic materials are easy to find and use, are naturally good insulators, and are non-toxic.

All of these different building materials have advantages and disadvantages that need to be carefully considered before using them in your home. The use of organic material, though very sustainable, may present a risk of decay. More durable materials may not be as ecologically friendly, but they do not need to be replaced or repaired as much. If you are working with a designer or architect, you may choose to let him or her decide which materials to use in your home. If you are doing it yourself, you will have to make the important choices. In any case, it is important to understand the advantages and disadvantages of these materials and how you would like to see them incorporated in your home.

Structural Designs

After you have come up with a buildable set of plans, the next step is a little more difficult. Your plans need to be structurally certified for construction by a licensed engineer. Unfortunately, a house plan is more than just deciding where rooms must go on a piece of paper. Earth-sheltered homes must be designed to carry the heavy earth loads that are imposed on them. Earth has significant weight, and wet earth is even heavier. These types of loads are not something a conventional home must deal with. Because of this, underground structures must be structurally designed for this special requirement.

Soil testing

As it turns out, designing a structure to carry the weight of earth is only part of the problem. The force of water, or hydrostatic forces, must also be accounted for. In order to hold back bermed earth, the structure must also hold back the water this earth contains. Acting somewhat like a dam, the water forces held by a house wall can be significant. These hydrostatic forces can be so significant that they actually cause a structural collapse or move a house from its foundation.

To make matters even more complicated, different types of soil can contain different amounts of water. This can make the hydrostatics forces unpredictable without first doing a soil test. The soil on your site must be tested to see how much water it can contain so that the structure can be engineered properly. Sand and gravel soils are the best draining soils, and clay and loamy soils are the worst. The better a soil drains, the less water and weight will have to be dealt with in your home design. Good draining soil is the ideal.

In some parts of the country, different soils are so bad that special precautions must be taken to protect structures from landslides and structural collapse. Clay soil in the rainy Northwest can sometimes create extreme slide hazards. Water-saturated soil trapped between a structure and the clay below it can create a slippery situation. Sometimes whole hillsides can literally slide away. My sister's family had a neighbor who knocked on their door at 3 a.m. after two entire stories of the house slipped 2,000 feet down a steep hill into Puget Sound. The neighbor had to climb out of a second story window to get out of the house because the downstairs floor was filled with mud. The disaster completely destroyed the family's uninsured custom dream home.

Thus, the engineering on your home design starts with a competent, licensed soils engineer. Good soils engineers can be found in the phone book. Ask for references and find someone you can work with comfortably. Test the soil first, and then a structural engineer, either working with your architect or directly for you, can help properly design the structure. A soils engineer will take careful samples and can examine all the soil on your property. This will help you design both the structure and the water drainage system.

Structural calculations

The next step in designing your home is to have a structural engineer look at your plans and certify that they will work. The structural engineering involves using math to calculate the size, composition, and placement of structural members in your home. Because of safety issues, these calculations must be done by a licensed professional. Structural engineers work either by themselves or in conjunction with an architect. You can find a local structural engineer in the phone book or online. Hourly rates usually run from $100 to $200 per hour. A typical residence can cost anywhere from $400 to thousands of dollars in engineering. If you have a set of working house plans, you must have it reviewed and stamped by a licensed structural engineer prior to submitting it for permit approval.

Permits and Fees

Once you have a set of working house plans that have been structurally certified, you can submit the plans to your local building code department for approval. Plan review and approval is usually a long process, depending on the complexity of the design. It can take anywhere from a few weeks to several months. If your plan uses any of the alternate or less conventional materials, review may take even longer. Be prepared to present documentation and answer any questions your building code official might have. The types of questions asked might include clarifications on sizes of doors or windows, or the grade or type of lumber used if they are not clearly spelled out on the plans.

Building materials, like earth bags, have been approved in some parts of the country, but are still a new idea in other areas. If you suspect your design of having any problems, be prepared to help educate your building code officials on all the intricacies of your building system.

Building code officials will carefully review your plans, looking at the structure, fire, plumbing, and electrical codes, as well as other important components of your plan. The plans you submit will come back approved, approved with corrections, or disapproved (most come back approved with slight corrections). Once you have your approved plans in hand, you are ready to begin construction.

CASE STUDY: COMFORTABLE DESERT LIVING

Dave Stoll, Carpenter and Earth-shelter Builder
6087 Dudley Drive
Mohave Valley, AZ 86440
www.pbase.com/deanne_123/earth_shel-
tered_home
undergroundcarpenter@gmail.com

David Stoll is a concrete form carpenter who has worked on large re-inforced concrete projects for hotels and casinos in the Las Vegas area. He built his own earth-sheltered homes about two years ago with poured concrete walls and a roof, and has been living comfortably in it ever since. He likes the fact that it is silent, fireproof, wind proof, termite proof, and maintains a constant temperature year-round. As for its greatest defect, Stoll lists that fact that his home is constantly at the same temperature, so is hard to change it even one degree. He also says earth shelters can limit your visibility to one direction only, which may bother some people.

Because he lives in the Mohave Desert, Stoll does not need any heat in the winter and spends little money cooling his home. His well water comes up at 92 degrees, so he does not even need a hot water heater.

Stoll's experience with permitting was exceptional. He had no trouble with approval and the inspections went smoothly. He said the structural engineer's stamp was the key to his success. Having a stamp made the plan approval a piece of cake.

Stoll used concrete to construct his home because that is what he is familiar with; however, he thinks other materials might work equally well. His plumbing and electrical systems were comparable to those in a conventional home, and went together without any problems.

For waterproofing, he used three-foot roles of peel 'n' stick poly "whatever" because it is inexpensive and readily available. Using materials that are available makes the builder's life much easier.

Dave said the biggest problem erecting an earth shelter is the fact that builders and subcontractors are unfamiliar with this type of home. Builers shy away from projects that are new to them, and they are not willing to learn the skills to become an underground homebuilder. Despite this, as a carpenter himself, he had no problems building one.

His home project was over budget, which he said is still a sore spot with his wife, but, he feels strongly that it is a great way to live. Quoting the late Malcolm Wells, the father of underground architecture, he reiterates the feeling that every square inch of the earth should be living. "Conventional homes leave a permanent dead footprint but earth-shelters are nurtured by being in harmony with the earth."

Planning for Construction

While your plans are being reviewed, it is a good time to begin working on the many elements of construction that require preparation. These include getting the site ready, finding contractors and subcontractors, and calculating building costs. If you are doing the project yourself, this is the best time to begin researching and learning all the construction skills you will need to build your home. Any education helps, even if you are not going to be doing the actual work yourself. Knowing how a plumber pipes a home may help you supervise your plumber.

At this point, a homebuilder would plan a master schedule of construction with all the key milestones for each construction phase clearly spelled out. *See Appendix A for more information on construction schedules.* He or she would be lining up subcontractors and calculating their true construction expenses. If you are building a home for yourself, you should be doing the same thing.

Estimating your building costs

Once you have a working set of plans, it is a good time to start calculating your construction costs to better plan your project. You will know how much you have to spend on each part of the project, and you will be able to keep control of construction costs as you build. This point was made clear to one homeowner, who was told by the ready-mix truck driver to watch every penny at the start of the project. This was sound advice. The poor driver had run out of money halfway through his project because he did not keep track of what he was spending.

Starting a house without having budgeted costs is like going to a store without a shopping list. It is too easy to buy things you do not need and come home with an empty wallet. More than one homebuilder has started with plenty of money, only to find that spending a little here and there has left him or her broke at the end of the project.

Project costs are sometimes difficult to estimate, even for an experienced builder, but knowing these costs as closely as possible will allow you to make important decisions. You will be able to estimate how much money you will need, when it will be needed, and where it can be best spent. If the project is too expensive, you will know at the start where you can save costs. By costing out your project, you will also learn where money should be spent to get the best return on investment. One example might be the use of a heat pump for heating, which might have a higher initial cost of installation, but be cheaper in the long run to operate. The planning stage is also the best time to save money on your project. The cost of your new home will depend on the complexity of the home design, the type and cost of materials used, and how much labor you do yourself. Thus, costs incurred by a complex design are best fixed in the design phase, but costs for labor and materials are best addressed in the planning phase.

Building a home involves thousands of choices, and almost all of these decisions involve money. Sourcing, pricing, and planning your project can be the biggest tools in its construction. A typical home has tens of thousands of items incorporated into it. A simple savings on even a few of these items can be a big step to making a home more affordable.

For example, alternative methods of construction, like earth bags, are extremely inexpensive, but have some preparation involved. Finding the best source for plastic bags is one of these necessary preparations. Metal framing is more expensive than wood framing, but may be worth the extra expense; however, this decision must be made prior to framing. Each decision that is made with confidence and research presents the best alternative to help your project run smoother.

Using a home building contractor

If you are contracting with a builder, calculating your building cost is quite easy — your cost will be the price on the contract signed by both you and the contractor. This should be a firm price that includes everything you need in your new home. It will be established during negotiations with the builder based on the plans and specifications you approve. Be careful to ensure that every detail is pinned down. You should have in writing everything that is important to you, even down to what type of light bulbs will be in each light fixture. If you do not, you may find no light bulbs are included in your light fixtures. Once you have a firm contract, you have a firm price. This will handle everything but construction changes.

Unfortunately, almost every project has changes. Good planning will eliminate most, but not all, changes. As you are building, you may discover the master bedroom must have a skylight, or the stone the builder selected does not look quite as good as the premium stone your spouse wants. Do not worry — changes in construction are inevitable. The trick is to make any change cost-manageable.

Most contractors add a change order fee for every change you make on the original drawings or scope of the work. In this way, a simple change like, "Gee, it would be nice to have a skylight in the master bedroom," can cost you thousands of dollars more. It is not uncommon to come to the end of a project and have the builder present a bill for tens of thousands of dollars' worth of small change orders that the owner had forgotten he or she even ordered.

The way to manage these changes is to build a contingency in your bid. Plan on slight changes and make sure you keep track of them as the building progresses. If you plan for $10,000 worth of changes, this becomes a part of your construction costs, which are allocated as the project progresses. If you run out of change order money in your budget, you can be more conservative in any changes. If you get to the end of your project with no money spent on changes, it is better than if you under-budgeted. It is better to plan for extra expense than be caught without money at the end of your project.

About 60 percent of customer complaints when working with contractors relate to scheduling problems; almost all of the rest relate to cost overruns. Make sure you have a strong agreement with your contractor about how change orders are handled. Do not trust that, because there is no change order agreement when the contractor adds the skylight in the master bedroom, you are going to get it for free. It never works that way.

Self-contracting

If you are your own contractor on your shelter, project costs will be a little harder to calculate. You will need to break your project up into bite-sized chunks and get pricing on each part. Start by deciding which parts of the project you will be doing yourself, and which parts you need help on. Owners in many states are allowed to do their own plumbing and electrical, as well as almost every other phase of construction. Some of these phases are more difficult than others, and you may wish for help on these parts. Generally, things like excavation, well drilling, concrete work, septic systems, framing, plumbing, heating, electrical, drywall, and interior finishes are tasks which might call for help from a professional. They usually involve special equipment or skills that have been learned with experience. But, all phases of home construction can be done by an owner given enough time and practice.

Start your cost estimate by getting a firm bid on everything you are having subcontracted. The general rule of getting three bids from subcontractors does not always have to be followed. The idea is to get the best price from the best-qualified subcontractor that you can work well with. The cheapest price is not always the best work. Make sure that you take the time to get to know the subcontractor and decide whether or not he or she is qualified to do the work. Make the subcontractor put everything in writing that is included and excluded by the contract, and check references to make sure the subcontractor can honor his or her commitments to time, quality, and price.

Becoming an owner and building contractor is a great way to save money. By contracting your home out, you are essentially saving the profit and overhead that would go to a contractor. There is, however, always some risk involved. The biggest risk is your inexperience. As a homebuilder myself, I always relish the thought of a new construction project challenge, but I learned a great deal in the first few houses I built. There was plenty of money wasted in practical, on-the-job homebuilding training. If this is your first project, you may also find this to be the case. Do not be afraid of the challenge; the construction process will cost you a little more in terms of time and money, but you will make it up in savings.

While the experienced contractor is going to be more efficient at construction, he or she also has to mark up materials and labor to cover the cost of doing business and the money he or she wishes to make on the project. The average net profit in the homebuilding business is probably about 10 percent of the contract price. General gross overhead and operating expenses for a home contractor can be in the neighborhood of 25 to 30 percent of the contract price by the time labor taxes and business expenses are paid.

When I constructed my own personal house several years ago, I had the advantage of a contractor's license to buy materials cheaper than a regular homeowner would. This was a great advantage. Many owners/builders take the extra step of getting a contactor's license so they can get at least a 10 percent discount on the materials incorporated into their house. This usually involves paying for a business license and the insurance your state requires for a contracting business. In some states, this process more than pays for itself, but in others it is not worth the effort. For example, a 10 percent savings on a $25,000 lumber package is a significant savings. Most subcontractors will also give steep discounts to owners/builders with a contractor's license.

If you are doing a large part of your own construction labor, you are also going to save money. About 20 to 30 percent of a home's expense is spent in construction labor. High labor rates on the specialty phases, like plumbing and electrical, make them exceedingly labor-intensive. By contracting yourself and using owner labor, you have the potential of saving up to 40 or 50 percent of your home cost. On a $200,000 home, that is a huge savings, sometimes enough to justify time off from regular work for the project.

Any labor savings on your home project also come off the top of the whole project, which means they are not taxed or paid off over time with interest. Interest expense on a mortgage over 30 years can sometimes be three times the initial cost.

After you have a firm price on your subcontractors, it is time to figure the cost of the things you are going to do. Start by calculating the materials that you will be using in your house. Do not be afraid to ask for help on this. Suppliers like lumberyards can help you do a take-off of all the lumber you will need, just like ready-mix companies can help calculate how much concrete you will need. You can even get help at most hardware stores for the type of plumbing and electrical materials you will need. Make a careful list of everything needed on your project. Make certain to include all the materials you will be using, and remember to include any wastage factors. Concrete contractors include a 10 percent wastage factor on any calculated concrete yardage they pour. This covers any errors that might be made in calculation, batching the ready-mix, or in the actual onsite form dimensions. Forms do not always conform to the exact size at which they are calculated, and a one-half inch bow in a form can easily eat up plenty of concrete. It has also been known to happen that some ready-mix may be spilled or lost during a pour, so it is always better to have extra than not enough. It is easier and less expensive to send a ready-mix truck back with one-tenth of a yard of unused concrete than it is to order another truck with a one-yard minimum and try and pour a wall with a cold joint. With some building materials, calculating waste is a little easier, as they have a built-in waste factor. Wood floorers usually have a 3 to 5 percent waste factor, and drywall contractors determine the waste by how many complex angles the job has.

An important part of your material pricing includes sourcing the materials. Find the best price for all your materials, and remember that not all sources are the same. Some lumberyards specialize in different types of lumber, so one vendor may have the best price on beams, but may not be the best source for wood studs. Do not be afraid to negotiate with sources for materials.

Look for builder supply companies that specialize in lower prices on building materials. Also look for good deals on rummage and surplus sales. Every year, some local rotaries have a rummage sale of doors and windows. These are windows and doors that may have been ordered in a wrong size or were not picked up by a contractor. They are donated to the Rotary group by local businesses as charity and sold for nickels on the dollar. In fact, my kitchen ceiling is made of vertical grain car decking that was recycled from a school 1,000 miles away. Do not be afraid to creatively explore alternate sources for materials, because when it comes to finding the best cost, sourcing is everything.

The final step in your cost estimate is to calculate the labor on your project. There are two ways to do this. You can guesstimate the time required for each part of your project and add up the hours. For example, if you believe the plumbing will take three weeks, this gives you 120 hours of labor. This will give you a fairly accurate number of labor hours if you guess the number of weeks correctly. You will then want to assign an hourly rate to each labor hour.

The second and best way to figure labor costs is to buy a unit price labor book at a local bookstore. These books, published by companies like RSMeans, provide a unit cost for labor in every part of the home construction process. They are what builders use to bid on a construction project. If you are pouring 20 feet of footing, all you have to do is look up the unit labor number for pouring footing. If the book says it takes 0.24 hours of labor per linear foot of footing and you have 200 feet of footing, it will take approximately 48 hours. What is nice about these unit prices is that they are usually accurate. The tables even contain allowances for running to the lumberyard when your level breaks or pouring footing in the rain.

Another thing to remember when you are calculating your labor expenses is that some projects may require help. By figuring your total labor, even if you are not paying yourself, you will know what you can afford on labor help and what you are saving. Knowing your labor hours will also help you schedule your project more effectively.

After you have calculated your labor, materials, subcontractor costs, and building costs, you are very close to having a complete cost on your project. The only other thing you need to include is a contingency for unknown expenses. This is money that the project may cost you if you run into problems, forget to catch a cost, or need to add something later. Banks generally factor in a 15 percent contingency on all construction loans to owners. Builders add from 5 to 20 percent on their calculated construction costs to cover contingencies. There is no hard or fast rule for what to add, so use what you think is safe. Remember that very few projects come in under budget. It is impossible for even the very best estimator to see every cost before the project is constructed.

Summary

Most established homebuilders have learned that one of the most important parts of home building is proper planning. Proper planning allows resources to be efficiently and effectively applied to the challenge of home construction. Thinking ahead will eliminate most the problems faced by the homebuilder. Even more importantly, saving money involves good planning. Every facet of the home's design has the potential to either add or save money. Planning ahead can also eliminate many of the headaches that make home construction more of a nightmare than a pleasure, leaving you to enjoy the building process as you select your site and begin to develop your alternative, eco-friendly home.

Chapter 4

The Good Earth: Site Development for an Earth-Sheltered Home

> *"Buy land, they're not making it anymore."*
> — *Mark Twain, American writer and humorist*

Selecting Your Site

Matching a home design to your building site can be both an art and a science. Before you buy any property, look at the elevation of the land and how it is naturally contoured. Look at the views and find the southern exposure. Next, look at how your property will accommodate all the outside amenities necessary to support your home, and ask yourself the following questions:

- How will I supply power to my site?

- Where will the well and drain field go if I need them?

- How will the driveway access my site?

- Where will I be able to park?

- Is there enough room for storage on the property?

These are just some of the questions that must be answered prior to building. When you are planning your property layout, take the time to ask others whose opinions you value to give a fresh perspective on lay of the land. Sometimes heavily wooded or brush-covered properties are difficult for the inexperienced person to read. When you find something that has potential and you like it, you will know.

Purchasing good land is sometimes difficult because some sites have been picked over by the time you have a chance to look at them. One strategy that has been used successfully is asking your real estate agent to show you marginalized land, or land that may have had some other use, but can be converted to a buildable property. Stay away from marshy, wet, and low-lying flood plains. Land that is seasonally flooded is a problem for a conventional home, but is even more of a nightmare with an underground home.

Another word of caution is to be careful of any land covenants that may restrict your activities on the land. Some developed land carries specific prohibitions from building certain types of structures, like mobile homes, geodesic domes, or earth shelters. Property covenants can sometimes severely restrict what you wish to do on a property. They can limit the height of a building, or even how it is arranged on a property. Make sure that all the necessary easements are there to allow utilities and road access to the land. Some rare properties have excellent property features but are completely landlocked by the properties around them.

Excavation and Site Work

Having a clear picture of what you wish to accomplish before excavation begins is important. Start with a detailed lot plan that shows the location and elevations of all the structures, wells, roads, septic systems, and any other important things on the property. Your lot layout should also include a drainage plan, the location of soil tests, and any septic tests that have been done on the property. With this in hand, you are ready to start clearing your property.

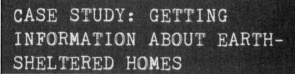

CASE STUDY: GETTING INFORMATION ABOUT EARTH-SHELTERED HOMES

Joel Akin
Earth House
93 Penmeadows PL SE
Calgary, Alberta, Canada T2A 3P8
www.earth-house.com
earthhouse@gmail.com

In 1997, I was searching the Internet looking for information on earth-sheltered homes and found very little information available. This was amazing to me because, since an early age, I have been interested in Mother Earth News and collecting information on sheltering and survival. I even wrote a report in the fifth grade with information that I collected, and it earned me an A+ on my report. When I loaned the information to a friend, he got an A on his paper, as well.

Collecting information in a central source can be of real help to people, and I like helping people. Because of this, I decide to start my own website with information on earth-sheltered housing. My site has more than 350,000 visitors every year who research earth-sheltered homes. It is a unique site with lots of information about underground housing, and even lists earth-sheltered homes that are for sale around the country. Though I have never built an earth-sheltered home or lived in one, I have had plenty of contact with people who have. My dream is to one day build and live in one myself.

Earth-sheltered homes are very different from conventional homes and require more planning. I see people on my website who sometimes run into trouble getting their dream homes built. They may have trouble finding a builder, getting mortgages, or dealing with a building problem for their underground homes. Though there are some good online earth shelter builder sites, there is still a general lack of good information online about earth-sheltered homes and financing. That is why my site tries to collect this information and disseminate it to the people who need it. What our country really needs is a North American self-funded organization that can build up and share information about earth-sheltered homes, and help people work out the kinks and twists that develop along the way. Such a resource would help get the government involved in this valuable process.

Britain has set up a governmental agency called the British Earth-Sheltered Association (BESA), which has made building earth shelters in that country much easier and more common. For a small fee, you can have access to all the information on this site, which includes public and private forums, photo galleries, surveys, resources, and links to other sites. This is an excellent resource and can be found at www.besa-uk. org.

There is a great wealth of information for people to learn about earth-sheltered housing, and more of it needs to be available. Valuable information on topics like siting a house, how to incorporate passive solar heating, how to insulate properly, and what resources are available for building and financing an underground home would be immensely beneficial. I am very interested in home designs that are "out of the box" — interesting and unique. I am fascinated by the concept of passive solar pit homes and super insulated homes that can stretch the limits of insulation to the theoretical limit of R-250 with vacuum insulation, but such ideas are still considered way out there.

From my experience, underground homes are comfortable, long lasting, and attractive alternative form of housing. Hopefully, I can help by getting information out there.

Land preparation

The land clearing process is different for every property and home design. It may consist of extensive land clearing with the removal of trees and brush, or simple grading to prepare the site for footings. Your land clearing can be done by a licensed excavation contractor, or you can do it with rented equipment. Operating excavation equipment is not easy and may require some practice. Always be extremely careful around heavy equipment, as it is easy for the equipment to get out of control. Once you have your equipment, getting a site ready for building involves several important tasks: land clearing, site drainage, wells, drain fields, and excavation for the building and footings.

When clearing land, remember to leave only the natural vegetation you wish to keep. This will make landscaping easier later. Brush can be removed, burned, or chipped into the property. Larger trees can sometimes be harvested for their timber, and money made from this can be used to help pay the cost of the land development. Take advantage of any special characteristics of the property by leaving unique natural features, such as large stones or special vegetation that add character to your land. Your land will have a much different feel after it has been cleared. If it is heavily wooded, you may find surprises. For most builders, getting the land cleared and seeing the true features is satisfying. For the first time, you will be able to see how your house will really sit on the property and how much excavation will need to be done.

Once your land is cleared, it is time to work on the site drainage. This may involve digging curtain drains in a hillside and filling them with gravel and pipe. It is important that site drainage begin as soon as you disturb the land. Vegetation stripped from the earth leaves the soil unprotected and subject to erosion and the collection of ground water. Use protective drainage fabric (silt cloth), hay bales, and temporary drainage to assure that your lot stays dry and protected even in the heaviest rains. Erosion control products can be purchase at any local lumber yard or building supply company.

Any wells you might need should be started as soon as your lot is cleared so water will be in place for construction. Another important item to install right away is a temporary electrical service. These simple posts, with power boxes and meter attached, can usually be purchased prefabricated at an electrical supply company or fabricated from scratch to match the local power company's specifications. Your state department of labor and industries (L&I) usually can supply a diagram of what type of configuration is acceptable for a temporary power post. Having power on site when you start your project is more of a necessity than a luxury. Many owners and builders even bring in temporary living accommodations or construction sheds at this point so they have somewhere out of which to work.

Another thing to think about at the start of your project is getting the septic drain field started if you have one. This usually begins by requesting a drain field design and having a perk test done on the property. In areas that have no sewer connection, however, the drain field acts as a disposal area of all of your house's septic wastes. These are the things that, if not properly handled, can make you sick. Human waste and grey water from your sink, dishwasher, or washing machine must be properly disposed of. In areas with no sewer connection, this is done by allowing the water to filter into the ground. A drain or septic field is where this happens. For it to happen the ground must be porous enough to allow this wastewater to filter away. Water goes from the house to a septic tank, which holds it and allows the solids to settle out. The water is distributed to the drain by gravity and filters away into the ground.

In order to assure the ground is porous enough to construct a drain field it is usually tested for its ability to percolate water. This is called a perk test. A perk test consists of several test holes being dug and filled with water to test the soil's ability to absorb water. You can usually find a good drain field designer who can do a perk test on your property in the phone book under "septic system design."

In some cases, lots do not pass the perk test. When this happens, very expensive drain field mound systems may be required. When these systems are built, a drain field is constructed on top of the existing ground. Such systems can be extremely expensive to build, so try and stay clear of lots that do not pass the perk test for this reason. Typical mounding systems can be in excess of 20,000 to 30,000 to construct.

The next steps include having a septic system designated and tested, and making sure there is a well started and power is on the site. By doing this, you can take the next steps to continuing your drainage plan. Make sure that all portions of the house are well-above the natural water table on the property, and that there are no natural springs or artesian wells under or behind the structure. Building near a river or on a flood plane is not a wise idea. Design your drainage system to drain everything down hill and make sure that you have more than enough extra capacity to handle stormy conditions or even 100-year floods. Your drainage plan should include provisions for water caught behind any berm walls, the footing drains, and roof drain-off. Sometimes it will be necessary to incorporate storm retention systems in the form of catch basins, or concrete structures that hold excess water, to ensure adequate capacity for periods of heavy precipitation.

As you install your drainage system, you can begin the building excavations. Of course climate, soil, and property conditions determine how you will excavate for a building. In some areas of the county, dynamite blasting is necessary to clear areas of rock ledge. In other areas, steep land slopes may have a tendency to produce landslides if not well-drained. Each area has its own idiosyncrasies.

Site differences

The best soil type for underground construction is a sandy or rocky soil that drains water easily. Be careful to avoid building in areas with a high concentration of clay, because problems can occur more easily. The smaller particles in clay hold much more water than other types of soil. This increases the hydrostatic pressure of the soil, which makes it heavier. In steeper areas, heavy water retention by the soil can produce a risk of landslides. In some areas of poor soil, you may even have to import better draining soil to use as backfill materials around your walls. Make sure that any home excavation you do is well-drained, even if temporarily. Cover your excavation material to keep it dry if you are planning on using it for backfill.

With the property properly excavated, you are now ready to layout your foundation structure on the property and get ready for the footing excavation. The layout of building will determine where the foundation goes. *The procedure for constructing the flooring will be explained in Chapter 5.* It is always wise not to excavate for the footings until you have a set of approved plans and are ready to form and pour it. Excavated footing trenches can collect rainwater, which can become a muddy mess by the time you are ready to pour. This collected water can wash out the correct elevations and make footings unlevel. When you have laid out your footings and are ready to excavate, you can use a machine to excavate to a rough grade, and then hand-excavate with a shovel to get the elevation more precise later. It is best to over-excavate around both the footing and the foundations to allow room to move around and work. Typically, four extra feet of "work room" is necessary to set forms and pour. Pay special attention at these points to the logistics of construction. Where will the ready-mix truck be able to sit when pouring the footing and foundation? Where will the lumber package be delivered? Answering these logistical questions now will make your job run more smoothly later.

Making a Bad Lot Better

Every lot is different and some lots are hard to clearly see until they have been cleared and the project has been laid out. Some lots fall under the heading of what is called marginalized land. Marginalized land is land that may have had an earlier use or has some feature that degrades it and makes it considered by some to be "not as good" as regular property. Examples of marginalized land include gravel quarries, small and odd shaped lots, lots next to power lines, or lots that have a peculiar location. In highly developed areas, these may be the only lots that are available to build on. Marginalized land can be a good deal if you look at it carefully. Some of the best deals can be had on property that others consider marginalized. A gravel quarry lot can offer well-draining soil with a pre-excavated building site. If the land you are looking at is marginalized, think creatively about what it is that makes it marginalized and how you can turn disadvantages into advantages. A friend of mine purchased a lot near power lines for one-third the cost of regular buildable property after he found out that the power company was going to go to an underground service in five years.

Another hint in the property development game is to look for property that may have an older structure that can be demolished and removed. In areas where property values escalate rapidly, it is a common practice to tear down existing homes and build new ones when the property values become worth more than the property with the building on it. An old, dilapidated building on the property might be considered a detriment to most people, but to the smart developer who plans on tearing the building down, the property might be perfect.

Summary

Getting a site ready for your new home can be a challenge. Clearing, excavating, and providing the proper amenities for construction can sometimes take a lot longer than you think. Every lot is different and you will never know what the lot is really going to look like until you have it cleared and graded. Look for good land but do not be afraid of making marginalized land better. The lot you build on might be where you will live for a while so choose wisely.

Chapter 5

On a Firm Foundation: Footing and Foundation Construction for an Earth-Sheltered Home

> *"A successful man is one that can lay a firm foundation with the bricks that others have thrown at him."*
> — *David Brinkley, American newscaster*

Concrete Construction

As discussed earlier, concrete is one of the most commonly used building materials. Using concrete involves forming, pouring, and stripping forms. The skills involved depend on the difficulty of the task. Pouring concrete involves calculating the amount of concrete needed, setting up forms, pouring the concrete, allowing the concrete to cure, removing or stripping forms, and completing final concrete finishes. Pouring concrete may also involve special additives and concrete testing.

The first step in pouring concrete is usually laying out and setting up the forms. It is very important that these forms be straight, level, and true. A house that starts off unleveled will only get worse by the time you get to the roof structure. The forms must also be strong enough to remain in place and hold the integrity of the form shape until the concrete has cured. If they loosen up during a pour, you will have real problems. Common problems include form shifting, form bowing, and concrete blowout, which will be discussed later in this chapter.

To order concrete, you must have the ability to calculate the amount of concrete needed. This involves a calculation of the area of your forms. A footing 2 feet wide by 1 foot high by 100 feet long has a calculated area of 2 feet by 1 foot by 100 feet, or 200 cubic feet. Professional concrete contractors usually add from 5 to 10 percent extra to cover wastage and form irregularities on the site. This means that if you have a job that requires 5 cubic yards of concrete, it is probably wise to order 5.5 yards on the truck. If you do not have the ability to calculate the amount of concrete necessary, a ready-mix company can help you with this calculation. Ready-mix concrete companies can be found in every area of the country. They supply concrete that is mixed in a truck and delivered to your building site. You will probably have more than a few in your area. Get competitive bids on the ready-mix you order because prices can vary significantly between different companies.

Most ready-mix trucks carry between 8 and 10 yards of concrete. If your project requires more than that you will need to order multiple truckloads. Multiple pours require that both trucks come one after another. Logistically, this makes the pour more difficult. Delays in a concrete pour can cause pouring irregularities known as cold joints, which decrease the structural strength of the final concrete.

Concrete ready-mix delivered to your site is usually given an allowable pour time based on the size of the load. If this pour time allowance is exceeded, hourly fees are added to the cost of the concrete. This means that it is important to have enough help when you are doing your pour to finish in the allotted time.

Footing Construction

A wise builder once told me that the whole integrity of a building depends on its footing. In a sense, this is true. If your footing is not square or level, your whole structure will also not be level. Little changes in the footing can be magnified by the time they reach the structure of the roof. If your footing is 2 inches off, this could mean a 4- to 6-inch problem by the time you construct the roof. Over the course of building your earth-sheltered home, make sure to spend extra time to ensure that the foundation is done correctly.

The foundation starts with a proper footing. A construction footing is merely a wide platform that allows the structure good bearing on the surrounding soil. The building codes in your area will tell you how wide and how deep the footing needs to be. Typical footing widths of 12 to 18 inches are common. Footing heights of 6 to 12 inches deep are also common. The size of your footing will be shown on your plans. Do not deviate from this size or the whole structural integrity of the building could be in jeopardy.

The footings can be poured with the foundation or separately. Pouring the footing separately can add a few hundred dollars to your project, but also makes the formwork and logistics more manageable. When the footing is poured at the same time as the foundation or the flooring, this is called a monolithic pour. A monolithic pour means all the concrete forms one continuous piece. Pouring the footing and foundation, or the floor and footing at the same time makes the pour more efficient and can save in curing time, but it also increases the complexity of the pour. If you do not have a lot of experience with concrete, it is probably wise to keep your pours as simple as possible.

The footing begins with a proper layout. This is done with stakes and careful measuring. The dimensions from the blueprint need to be translated into an actual structure on your property. Builders will sometimes start on a corner of the building with something called a corner board or batter board. This allows them to square off the structure from one corner and stake, measure, and square the whole building. Corner boards are nice tools, but they are not always necessary; most footings can be laid out carefully by measuring and squaring the structure with two people, a tape measure, and wood stakes.

The general tool for laying out a footing consists of a 100-foot-long tape, a string line, wooden stakes, and a level. Careful measuring translates the dimensions of your footing to the property. The footing depth will be determined by the frost line in your area. The deeper the frost penetrates the ground, the deeper the footing will have to be. In the Pacific Northwest, this means most footings are 12 to 18 inches below grade. In Maine, footings may be 2 feet below grade. In the warmer southern parts of the country, footings can be poured right on the surface of the ground. In any case, the footing should lie on undisturbed ground. It should be constructed so that is it is level and square.

Leveling can be achieved by hand-excavating the footing to grade and then using a level. A new tool called a hose level will also allow you to level all parts of the footing at the same time. A transit can also be used to level all points from a standard position. Hose levels and transits can be rented from a construction rental company. Both will save time in the leveling process. If you are having trouble leveling the ground, this can sometimes be compensated for by shimming and leveling the forms. Shimming can be done by placing wedge shaped boards under the bottom of the footing form to level the form. The key is that the top of the footing needs to level everywhere.

Squaring the footing is achieved by measuring from opposite corners and making sure the dimensions of one diagonal match the dimensions of the other diagonal. For example, if your house is a square measuring 20 feet by 30 feet, the dimensions from one corner of the house to the opposite corner diagonally should be roughly 36 feet. This dimension should be the same as the measurement from the diagonal formed by the opposite corners. If it is not, you can adjust the layout of the footing until both diagonals match. When both diagonals match, the footing is square.

Some builders take advantage of modern transit and laser leveling equipment. Transits are small telescopes that allow you to sight-in the levels between two points. Laser levels allow you to level something with the flat beam of a laser. Both tools create a very level measurement. This is an excellent way to save time and ensure your structure is level and square. Transit and laser leveling equipment can be rented at most rental stores. With a little bit of training, anyone can become proficient using this type of equipment. It can save time and ensure greater accuracy than laying your footing out by hand.

Once you have the footing properly staked, the next step is to construct the footing forms. Most builders use standard 2-inch by 6-inch or 2-inch by 8-inch framing lumber for their forms. This lumber will create the outside edge of your poured footing. The forming lumber for footings can be held in place by wood or metal stakes. Wood stakes can be cut from scrap lumber. Metal stakes can be rented from most rental stores. It is also common practice to hold the footing forms together with metal form ties on the top of your 2-inch by 6-inch or 2-inch by 8-inch forms This keeps the forms from spreading when you pour them full of concrete. These metal ties can also be used to support your foundation forms if you are pouring the foundation wall at the same time as the footing.

Footings can also be formed out of hard ground by excavating the size of the poured footing down from grade. The dirt sides of your form will be the sides or the footing. Excavated footings usually require more concrete than a wood-formed footing, but require less forming expense. If you are pouring your floor at the same time as the footings, you will have to frame the outside of the footing only. Pouring the footing and the floor at the same time will be discussed under the floor pouring section later in this chapter. Pouring the floor and the footing at the same time requires more expertise than pouring the footing separately.

Prior to the placement of any concrete, most building departments require a footing or foundation inspection. This usually requires two to three days for an inspector to be notified, inspect the forms, and leave notification that forms can be poured. Having a building inspector examine your forms before your pour ensures that the dimensions and elevations are acceptable to the building department. It does not ensure that the forms are level, square, or strong enough to hold the concrete. This must be done by you or your contractor. Most builders have more than one person inspect the forms for integrity before they pour. If you have a friend who is knowledgeable about forming concrete, this is a good time to ask for help.

If you are pouring the foundation after the footing, you may want to take advantage of installing a keyway in your footing. The keyway is a wedge-shaped trench in the top of the footing that helps keep the foundation on the footing. It also increases the bearing on the footing for lateral loads.

Keyway Drawings

Keyways can be formed in the top of the footing by inserting a well-oiled, wedge-shaped piece of lumber into the middle of the top of the footing form. This can be held in place by the footing form ties.

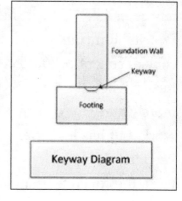

If you do not install a keyway, the footing reinforcement should be bent up into the foundation wall per building code. The footings are generally reinforced with steel rebar. The amount of reinforcement will depend on your local building code. Typically, two pieces of

½-inch reinforcing are run continuously through the footing, and this same bar is bent up every 2 feet into the foundation.

Footing Drawing

Once your footing forms are secure and inspected, you are ready to pour the footing. Be sure to remember to order 5 to 10 percent extra concrete for your pour. Typical footing and foundation concrete mix designs call for 3,000 to 4,000 PSI concrete. This is sometimes referred to as a four to six sack mix. Four to six sack mix means

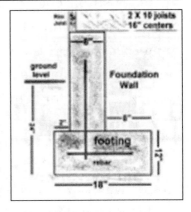

four to six sacks of cement to every yard of concrete. Your local ready-mix company usually has standard mix designs for footing and foundation wall constructions. The amount of water in your concrete will determine how easy it is to place. Water content is usually gauged in terms of the slump of the concrete — typical slump may be 3 to 5 inches. This means that a formed cone of concrete would collapse, or slump, anywhere from 3 to 5 inches when the form is pulled away. The higher the slump, the more watery the concrete is. Watery concrete is easier to pour and work, but has less strength after it is cured. Ideally, you want to keep the slump as low as possible, but high enough to be able to work the concrete easily into every area of your footing. It is better to order the concrete with less water at the start and gradually add water if it is too stiff to work properly. You can usually have the truck driver add water as you pour.

Ready-mix concrete also has many additives that can be placed in your concrete to improve its plasticity, strength, curing time, and resistance to cold. Most of these additives result in greater expense to the concrete and are not commonly used in residential construction.

One additive that may be worth considering, however, is called fly ash. Fly ash is an inexpensive ash material that can be added to concrete to improve its strength and decrease the amount of cement added. Adding fly ash to concrete can significantly increase its strength and reduce its cost per yard. The costs on a yard of concrete using fly-ash additive can be about five percent less with the same concrete strength. If you are not experienced with concrete additives, the best place to start is by talking with your ready-mix concrete supplier.

Pours that occur during exceedingly cold or warm weather may also need additives. Cold weather pours sometimes use an accelerant that causes the concrete to harden faster. Warm weather pours sometimes use a chemical retardant or ice to cause the concrete to harden slower and be workable longer.

The footings can be poured directly from the back of a ready-mixed truck or, for small jobs, from a mixer with a wheelbarrow. Concrete poured in the footing can be consolidated by screeding, or leveling, the concrete with a board to the top of the footing forms. Pouring times should be figured at about one-half of an hour to every yard of concrete ordered. A typical footing may involve 4 to 8 yards of concrete. It would take about one and one-half to three hours for three people to pour a footing like this.

Because footings are so critical, allow extra time and manpower to make sure everything gets poured correctly.

Curing time should be at least two to three days before the footing forms are removed. Form removal should go quickly. Make sure that the footings are scraped clean while the concrete is still soft and green. Curing time for the footing should be at least one week before the foundation is poured on top of it. If your foundation is poured separately, it will have to be laid out on top of the footing and squared separately.

Foundation Construction

One way to save money pouring your footing and foundation is to pour them both at the same time. Foundation forms can be placed on top of footing forms and both can be poured as a solid monolithic pour. In the old days, foundation walls would be poured with board on board forms. This is why foundation walls poured more than 60 years ago still shows the imprint of the boards that were used to form them. Today, foundation form technology has come a long way. Special clips allow the builder to set reusable forms for a foundation. Plywood foundation forms can be attached together as easily as an Erector set. With simple instructions and the correct forming materials, a foundation wall can be set up quickly and easily.

Foundation-forming materials can be rented from stores or companies that specialize in renting foundation materials. Form rental companies can look at your blueprint and tell you exactly what forms you need. The forms will be delivered to your site and picked up when you are done. Form rental is typically five days to one week, which allows the forms to be set up, inspected, poured, and set for several days while the concrete hardens. Most companies require the forms to be well oiled with releasing oil prior to pouring and well-cleaned prior to form return.

Foundation forms are usually erected on top of the metal spread plates that hold the footing forms together. The form rental company can help you with this. Foundation forms are erected at a starting point on one end of the building and are connected by working your way around the structure. Like footing forms, foundations forms should always be placed sufficiently below grade to avoid any problems with freezing or frost heave. In colder areas of the country, the ground can actually move up to 12 inches as it freezes. Frost heave is avoided in these areas of the country by being cast below the freezing level and by insulating properly.

Once erected, your foundation forms will need to be inspected by the building department. They will also need to be checked to make sure that they are secure and will not fail to hold the concrete during the pour. The most common problem during concrete pours is something called "blowout." A concrete blowout occurs when the weight of concrete pulls the forms apart, which can create a huge mess. Concrete is a heavy material and filling forms with concrete creates very large stresses on the forms. When the forms do not hold together properly, concrete will blow out everywhere. When this happens, many yards of concrete may have to be moved out of the way while the forms are reconnected properly. The reconstructed forms will then have to be re-poured. While you are setting up your forms, the reinforcing material for your foundation wall must be placed in the form so that it can be incorporated into your poured wall. The type of reinforcement will depend on the height, width, and structural loading on the wall. Typically, ½-inch rebar is placed on 2-foot centers vertically and horizontally. Your building plans should have the reinforcement requirements on them, and form rental facilities can usually provide the reinforcement needed for your project.

Foundation reinforcement photo courtesy of Earth Shelter Technologies, Inc.

As you are pouring the foundation wall, standard practice is to vibrate the concrete into place using an appliance called a concrete stinger or sting vibrator. This is a handheld vibrating tool

that has a long flexible rod that can be inserted into the foundation wall. The concrete stinger allows you to vibrate and consoli-
date the concrete in your forms. It assures that there will be no
hollow cavities or air holes in the poured wall. It is standard practice to pour a foundation wall in 2-foot to 3-foot lifts. This means
that you would start at one end of the foundation and pour 2 feet
up the forms and move all the way around the foundation before
pouring the next 2 feet. These lifts, or layers, of concrete are consolidated using a concrete stinger vibrator, and then the next 2- to
3-foot lift is poured.

Once the foundation wall is poured completely, the top surface
is screeded, or brushed flat with a flat trowel or wood board. It
is important to remember at this point to insert any bolts or reinforcing material into the top of the foundation wall while the
concrete is still soft. Building code usually requires the placement
of galvanized J bolts into the top of a foundation wall to provide
an attachment for framing. These bolts, which are more L shaped
than J shaped, will stick up about 2 inches above the foundation
wall and provide an attachment for any wall framing. If the roof
structure is poured or precast panels are added later, they will tie
into reinforcing coming up the foundation walls. This reinforcement will need to be in the walls and extending above the walls
to tie into the roof concrete.

Poured foundation walls for earth-sheltered homes are sometimes much taller than regular foundation walls because most
of the house sits below the ground. Walls poured against dirt fill
can be 8 to 10 feet tall. The taller the wall, the more difficult it will
be to pour. Two-foot foundation walls are much simpler to pour
than 8-foot foundation walls. If you are pouring tall or more dif-

ficult walls, you might require professional help. Some concrete contractors will actually hire out the day of the pour to help you with the hardest parts. Another option to get help is to run an ad in the local paper asking for someone with concrete pouring experience to help you with your project.

Because foundation walls require more concrete, the pour time and complexity increases. Typical foundation pours can sometimes entail more than one concrete truck, and it is important that all concrete be poured continuously to prevent cold joints from forming. Make sure that you allow for enough labor to help during the pour process. A foundation wall 8 feet high and 200 feet long would require a minimum crew of four to five people to pour. Working with less help has a potential to get you into trouble if you run into any problems.

Once the foundation wall is poured, allow two to three days for the concrete to cure and harden before removing the forms. Once the forms are removed, it is an excellent time to cut form ties, scrape and clean the foundation wall, and patch any holes or voids. Use a non-shrinking epoxy ground to patch any holes or voids. Surface blemishes and irregularities can be scraped off with a sanding stone block. Right after the forms are stripped, the concrete is still very soft and can be cleaned much more easily during this time period. Builders sometimes forget to take this extra step at this point to clean their foundations. The voids and marks on concrete will become more visible later and be almost impossible to correct after the concrete becomes hard.

Pouring the footing and foundation wall at the same time will save you all the time necessary to screed the footing. It also streamlines the process of setting up and stripping the forms. Although pouring both at the same time increases the complexity of your project, it also can save you money.

Good curing time for the foundation wall can be anywhere from one to three weeks, depending on the temperature and type of loads of the building. If you are in a big hurry to begin construction on a poured wall, test the concrete. The strength of your concrete wall can be determined by pouring test core samples at the same time you pour the wall. Test core samples consist of approximately 6-inch round by 12-inch high plastic forms that are filled with concrete and then crush tested after curing to determine the strength of the concrete. The core sample forms can be obtained from any concrete testing laboratory, and they can do the testing for you. Concrete strength can also be determined by several instruments that are designed to test ping the concrete and determine its strength. Test pinging involves a small pin that "pings" or hits the concrete. The strength of the concrete can then be determined by how deeply the pin penetrates the pour. Concrete will continue to cure and get harder virtually forever. The best method of providing enough strength is to be patient and allow sufficient curing time.

It goes without saying that the concrete must be hard enough to allow backfill before you backfill. Some of the biggest problems occur when builders become too eager to backfill against a concrete wall that is not yet hard enough. Backfilling against a concrete wall adds thousands of pounds of stress on the wall. If you fill too early the wall has the potential to collapse. Before you do the backfill, make sure that the wall is strong enough to handle the extra load of weight.

Flooring

Not all earth-sheltered home residents need or want a concrete floor. Other options include earth or wood. Building codes do not require a concrete floor, but a concrete floor has many advantages. It is attractive, strong, and durable. Concrete floors can be easily cleaned and come in a variety of finishes. Concrete can be left in contact with earth surfaces, whereas wood floors need to be elevated and protected from contact with dirt. For this reason, concrete is probably the most popular choice for the first-story floor of a home.

Floor reinforcement photo courtesy of Earth Shelter Technologies, Inc.

Pouring a concrete floor is in some ways much more difficult than pouring the footing and foundation. One of the things that makes it more difficult is that the floor is a finished surface that will be exposed to view. Some owners who choose to pour the footing and foundation walls subcontract floor pouring to ensure a high-quality finish and a level floor. The most common type of floor slab is called the slab on grade. The slab on grade is poured over native ground material that has from 6 to 18 inches of sand or gravel fill over it. When placing this fill, it is important to provide the correct compaction and leveling. Leveling can be done with the use of leveling stakes and a transit. Compaction is usually done with the use of a machine vibrating compactor or water-filled roller. The outside of the slab fill is usually thinner than the center fill. This provides for drainage away from the exterior walls. One to 2 inches of hard board insulation is usually installed under the slab 2 to 4 feet from the perimeter. This perimeter insulation provides additional temperature protection. Some floor slabs include the use of a 4- to 20-mil polyethylene vapor barrier under the slab. The mil thickness of the polyethylene specifies its thickness. One mil is .001 inches or one thousandth of an inch thick. This provides an extra level of protection from water infiltration through the floor slab. Most floor slabs are poured without reinforcement. When they are reinforced, it is usually with the use of a galvanized wire mash fabric. This is similar to animal cage material and can be purchased at the same places where rebar reinforcement is sold. It is also important to pour any internal footings required for structural support on the interior of your slab. This can be done by digging a deeper hole for the footing in the areas where structural-roots support is required. These areas definitely require reinforcing. Floor slabs are usually poured to a nominal thickness of 4 inches. Because common screed boards are 2 feet x 4 feet, the actual thickness of a floor slab is usually closer to 3 ½ inches.

Many modern structures include in-floor heating and utilities. If your plan calls for utilities for heating in or below the floor structure, this will need to be addressed while you are pouring the floor. *The installation of these utilities will be discussed in Chapter 6.*

When you are pouring your floor separately, use the foundation wall as the outside of your floor form. Place a level line mark on the foundation wall, which will provide a mark for your slab. The secret to pouring a concrete floor slab is creating a level and smooth, finished surface. The slump or stiffness of concrete for the floor slab should be higher than the stiffness of the concrete ordered for your foundation wall. Generally, a large floor structure is divided up into smaller areas that are formed by temporary screed boards. A screed board is typically a board that is the thickness of your slab. For a 4-inch slab, two-by-fours form an excellent screed board. Screed boards are staked temporarily in the middle of your slab in 8 to 10-foot increments. *See following screed diagram.*

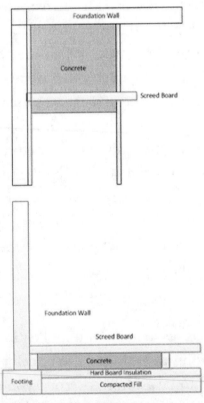

Screed Diagram

The concrete is placed between the screed boards and raked roughly level with a straight 2 by 6 or medal screed that is pushed over the top surface of the screed boards. As it is pushed, the concrete is leveled in front. Proper screeding is a bit of an art. It requires two people who have a good feel for how quickly to push the concrete while vibrating and pulling the screed board back and forth.

Screeding brings the concrete to a level point. After it is leveled, the screed board is removed and concrete is poured in the void that remains. Concrete is placed in the floor starting at one end of the structure, and you work to the opposite side, screeding the concrete level as you go.

After the concrete is screeded, the next process involves floating the concrete to a smooth finish. This can be done on smaller slabs with a large floating trowel called a bull float. A bull float is pulled along the top of the floor while the concrete is still wet to bring the fine material in the concrete to the surface. Bull floats are usually made of aluminum or magnesium for easy traveling. They have extension handles that enable you to reach 12 to 15 feet into your slab at one time. The bull float is run over the finished slab before it hardens to create a smooth, flat surface. You can rent a bull float at any rental store.

The concrete needs to be troweled after it is floated. This can be done with the use of hand trowels, but a power trowel should be used with larger slabs. Power trowels look like large upside down fans. Each fan blade consists of a trowel surface that spins and finishes the concrete. Again, finishing concrete requires some degree of practice and skill. The larger the pour, the more concrete that needs to be finished before it hardens. Some concrete finishing contractors will subcontract only the finishing part of the floor work and charge you a flat fee per square foot for finishing. If you do not have experience with concrete or are unsure of your abilities, this is a good option to consider. You will get the clean finish of a concrete finisher without having to pay a contractor to do all the concrete work.

The final step in pouring the slab sometimes includes a curing agent and sealer applied to the floor to ensure the proper curing and finishing. A curing agent is a chemical that helps the concrete harden smoothly and properly. The curing agent is usually sprayed on the slab with a garden sprayer after the concrete has been finished, but before it becomes hard.

The sealer is a chemical that revives the finished look of the concrete slab. The sealer is usually applied the same way as the curing agent after the concrete has hardened and cured. Sealers are applied the day after the pour. They can be flat, semi-gloss, or gloss finish. This will determine what the final concrete of the floor looks like if your final floor is finished concrete with no carpet or other floor covering. Be sure to use a quality concrete curing and sealing compound. This will ensure that the floor has an even finish.

Another alternate finish that can be applied to a concrete floor slab is called exposed aggregate. This is a very attractive concrete finish that shows the rock or aggregate in the surface of the concrete. The exposed aggregate method is relatively easy and inexpensive to do. The cost of doing an exposed aggregate finish is only about 5 percent more that a regular concrete finish.

Exposed aggregate finishes involve spraying a concrete retarding agent on the finished floor before it cures, typically after the floor has been troweled. The retarding agent can be a commercial product, or simply sugar water. Many concrete finishers use soda as the retarding agent spray because it is so high in sugar content. The retarding agent will keep the cement in the concrete from setting up on the surface of the slab. After the slab cures, the concrete can be pressure-washed to expose a beautiful rock finish. If you are planning on using an exposed aggregate finish, order concrete ready-mix with a higher aggregate or rock content. Concrete can be ordered with extra pea gravel or $\frac{7}{8}$ inch rock to provide for a beautiful rock finish. Your ready-mix supplier should have a good concrete design of aggregate finish on file. After the aggregate finish of your slab is exposed, seal it with a flat or glossy finish.

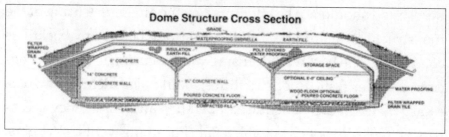

Drawing courtesy of Earth Shelter Technologies, Inc.

Roof Structures

The roof structures of underground homes can also be poured with concrete or installed using precast concrete panels. Pouring a roof for an earth-sheltered home is considered a very complicated and difficult task. Critical to the process of pouring a roof structure is providing temporary structural support for the pour and also supporting it while the concrete cures. In poured office buildings, this support is usually provided in the form of temporary wood or steel posting between floors. Roof structures can be poured over braced wood forms the same way a floor slab is poured. The critical element here is tying in the proper support for the wall system and structural support posts. Reinforcing systems from the walls must follow through into the roof support system, and structural support posts with footings must be constructed on the interior of the structure. Temporary structural bracing should remain in place until the roof structure has cured sufficiently to support the weight. Modern poured roof structures are often poured as a dome to create additional strength in the arch. Complex concrete roof structures can be poured or precast with hollow core or post-tensioning systems.

All of these systems involve a high degree of casting skill and expertise and should not be attempted by the amateur. Curing of the roof structures should be sufficiently strong before any backfill is conducted. The best way to ensure proper curing is through concrete cylinder tests. Roof structures should also include any necessary penetrations or required openings and emergency access panels. Not all roofs are totally flat. Plumbing vents, skylights, stove vents, and even TV antennas sometimes must penetrate through the roof structure. Any protrusions need to be properly flashed and waterproofed because they are the most vulnerable point for water penetration.

Summary

The foundation of a home lies quite literally in the construction of its footing and foundation. Constructing the proper footing, one that is level and true, will keep the rest of the house also level and true. Concrete is the essential ingredient for footing and foundation construction. Because of this, learning how to pour or cast concrete is essential to building your home. The more a person pours concrete, the better they become at it. The art and science of pouring concrete is a continuous learning process. Never be afraid to seek outside expertise advice when it is needed, particularly when learning how to cast concrete.

Chapter 6

Wired for Success:
Installing Your Utilities

"We will have solar energy as soon as the utility companies solve one technical problem — how to run a sunbeam through a meter"
— Anonymous

Home Utilities

Installing the utilities in an earth-sheltered home is very similar to installing the utilities in a conventional home, except it requires a bit more planning. Plumbing, electric, and radiant heat systems can all be installed in the slab floor. Limited access to walls in some areas may require surface-mounted conduit electrical and embedded plumbing or light fixtures. Installing plumbing, electrical, and heating in or under a concrete floor can be more difficult than installing below a suspended wood floor. Installing utilities below or in concrete can also make mistakes more difficult to correct. Proper planning and layout of the utilities prior to pouring the concrete floor is essential. Installing drain fixtures, electrical wiring, and heating fixtures in the floor requires precise layout.

Electrical Work

Some of the most important work in your new house will be the electrical work. Like the nerves controlling the vital parts of the body, the electrical system of your house will control the lighting, appliances, and in some cases the heating of your home. Wiring a house is also one of the most difficult elements of construction, one that many builders wisely choose to subcontracted out.

Because the electrical portion of your house is also one of the biggest expenses, you may choose to learn how to do your own wiring. Most states allow owners/builders to do their own wiring. Because of the highly technical labor, this is an area in which a great deal of money can be saved. If you desire to wire your own house, the first step is to do a fairly detailed takeoff from the plans of everything you will need for the rough wiring. The rough wiring includes wiring, switch boxes, plug-in boxes, light fixtures, and everything else necessary to provide the backbone of your electrical system. If you are having trouble figuring out what materials you need, many of the local hardware stores can be quite helpful. Weekend electricians are often found wandering the isles of these stores asking advice on the best materials to use and how to install them. Some of the larger home building supply companies can tell you what size wiring you need, direct you to all the necessary switch and outlet boxes, and even help you pick out the correct service panel boxes.

Rough Electrical Wiring

The rough wiring of your house will usually begin after the roof structure is on and everything is "dried in." This means there is no potential for a sudden rainstorm to get any electrical wiring wet. After you have assembled the materials, the next step is to mark where all the fixtures will go in your house. The layout markings will include the location of switches, electrical outlets, light fixtures, heavy appliances, and anything that needs to be connected to the electrical system. The plans should show the two-dimensional (2-D) location of electrical outlets, light switches, and light fixtures. The elevations of these boxes are determined by state electrical codes. In most states, the Department of Labor and Industries will do an inspection of your rough electrical work before you cover it to make sure it is all to code. All rough electrical will run through the stud partition walls on interior walls. In the ceiling, wiring will be surface mounted in conduit to the ceiling structure or run through a suspended or false ceiling.

Because underground homes may have some areas that are not easily accessible, particularly exterior walls made entirely of concrete, more of the electrical may have to be embedded in the floor or run as surface-mounted wiring in a conduit on the concrete wall. Alternate construction materials may require some creative embedding and conduit work. Construction materials, such as earth bagging, cordwood, and Earthship construction may require special considerations for the electrical wiring. When stringing wiring through the house, it is important to pay attention to any applicable building codes. These codes will dictate how high the switch boxes and electrical outlets must be placed above the floor. They will also dictate what type of materials must be used.

Local building codes will determine how many outlet boxes must be provided in each room, the size and wattage of lighting, and how large the service panel must be. Home service panels usually include a provision for 200 amp service. This is the typical amount of power that will be running to a home. Wiring must be sized for the applicable electrical demand loads. Rough electrical wiring can also become more complicated when the source of power is an alternate one, such as solar roof panels or wind power. Other considerations must be made if the site is in a remote location and alternate power systems like back-up generators or battery power system are used. Some earth-sheltered housing is designed to be totally off-grid with self-sufficient utilities.

The final step after the rough wiring is laid out is to actually place the boxes and wiring. This may entail some drilling, pulling of wire, and securing wiring and boxes. The purpose of rough wiring is to place all the electrical fixtures and wiring that will be covered up by wall treatments before the wall treatments go on. Though the mechanics of rough electrical wiring in earth-sheltered homes is not much different than wiring a conventional house, the differences primarily lie in finding an acceptable location for the wiring to pass. When in doubt, ask for help. Because of external lighting constraints in underground housing, it is wise to include more internal lighting than is necessary according to building code. Using full spectrum light bulbs will also help provide more natural light inside the home.

Remember: Another very important part of the electrical wiring of your home is to include provisions for any low-voltage systems that may be required. This includes systems like cable television, phone lines, Internet connection lines, and alarm and intercom systems. These systems are usually not diagrammed on a regular set of building plans. But, it is well worth the time to make provisions for these systems. Having them present in the modern age adds function and value to your home and increases its resale value.

Finished electrical

Once the rough electrical wiring, plumbing, and heating are completed, any interior walls are ready for cover. Electrical finish work is one of the last things to be done, and includes the installation of light fixtures, switch plates, and outlet plate covers. Finish work usually occurs after all the interior walls have been painted and flooring has been installed. By the time you get to your finished electrical, most of the decisions about how to finish should have been decided, and you may have even purchased all the electrical appliances that you need to install.

One of the hardest decisions to make in finishing the electrical work is what type of lights to install. A wide spectrum of options exists. Tracked lighting, drop lighting, recessed lighting, and surface-mounted fixtures can all be used. There is also a wide variety of light fixtures. These come in many different sizes and shapes, and will also match many different expense accounts. Large supply stores that solely specialize in lighting and electrical fixtures are the best places to educate yourself on what you will need. Unfortunately, it seems like the more choices there are, the harder the decisions are to make. Another good way to pick finished light fixtures is by consulting with your architect or looking at other homes and deciding what you like.

Saving money on electrical work

Because earth-sheltered homes are very energy-efficient, it is wise to install the most efficient electrical lighting and appliances in your new home. Modern, efficient light bulbs are more expensive to install, but last much longer and will save on energy resources. GE's new Energy Smart bulbs last ten times longer and save a maximum of 75 percent more energy than regular incandescent light bulbs, but they are 14 times more expensive. Factoring the energy and life savings per smart bulb, they save $34 each over the life of the Energy Smart bulb.

As mentioned earlier, it is also wise to include full-spectrum light bulbs so you can make up for the lack of natural daylight.

The biggest energy hogs in your new home will be refrigerators, hot water heaters, washers and dryers, and any other large appliances. To save money on the larger appliances, carefully review the sales literature that comes with them. There is a big difference between different brands of refrigerators as far as how much power each one uses. You may find that a conditional investment of a little more money for the appliance will save you money later in energy consumption. Another large source of electrical energy consumption in your home is the washer and dryer system. If your home has access to natural gas or propane, this will save money on not only these appliances but also on cooking.

Another clever way to save money on the electric system of your underground home is to let a licensed electrician do the rough electrical, and do the finish work yourself. Finishing the electrical is usually broken out as a separate item on most electricians' subcontractor bids. It can amount to about one-quarter of an electrician's bid. This work does not require a high degree of skill. Screwing on light switch plates, outlet plates, and installing finished light fixtures is easy to do. Money can also be saved by installing inexpensive light fixtures initially and trading them for more expensive ones later. Final permit approval usually does not require all light fixtures to be installed.

Saving money on appliances

One of the best ways to save money on your new underground home is to find a good source for all necessary appliances. Appliances, such as refrigerators, dishwashers, washers, and dryers are very expensive when purchased through a local retail outlet. One of the first things I discovered as a homebuilder is that appliances can be purchased through local builder outlets much less expensively. Many companies like Sears and Westinghouse have special dealer outlets designed specifically for building contractors. Such outlets offer appliance discounts in the range of 20 to 40 percent, and sometimes even more. Large homebuilders sometimes purchase appliances by the trainload, saving significant money from the home appliance package. Having a contractor's license or business license when you build your home may entitle you to a builder's discount on appliances. It is certainly something worth considering and researching carefully when you get around to buying your appliance package. Typical home appliance packages can run anywhere from $3,000 to $4,000. Thus, a 20 to 40 percent discount on this amount represents a significance savings if you can use your license.

Plumbing Work

Although the electrical system of a house can be compared to the nervous system, the plumbing system might be compared to a circulatory system. House plumbing does all of the heavy work. Plumbing carries the vital supplies of hot and cold water to the home, and more importantly, it carries away all of its waste products.

Interestingly, more human lives have been saved by the sanitary aspects of modern plumbing than by any other modern technological or medical development. Yes, you heard that right; plumbers have actually saved more lives than doctors.

It is estimated that 10 percent of the disease burden of society has been eliminated by the use sanitary plumbing. This has probably accounted for saving billions of lives in the modern era. Unfortunately many underdeveloped countries still are suffering from poor sanitation.

Before sanitary plumbing and water systems, epidemic waves of cholera, typhoid fever, and yellow fever periodically swept through massive sections of the human population. One interesting read discusses this proposition in the book *Flushed: How Plumbers Saved Civilization* by W. Hodding Carter. Many of us have never given plumbers the respect they deserve.

Despite the importance of plumbing, it still remains one of the most under rated building elements — house plumbing is usually considered the last thing of importance in a house until something goes wrong with it and then we can be up to our eyeballs in trouble.

Earth–shelter plumbing sometimes involves casting plumbing lines in or below a concrete floor slab, and this floor slab can sometimes be 8 to 10 feet below grade. Fixing a leaking pipe is hard enough when it is under a slab. When it is below a slab and deep below grade, fixing a leak can be not only difficult, but very expensive. This is why it is very important to make sure any plumbing installed in an underground home is done right.

Rough Plumbing

Aside from the electrical, rough plumbing is the second most technically difficult system in your house. Because of this, many owners and builders consider this a subcontract item; however, most states allow owners to do their own plumbing, and plumbers can be quite expensive by the hour. An inquiry into current Seattle plumbing rates turned up a figure of $31.25 per quarter hour, which is an hourly rate of $125 per hour. Most plumbers charge the minimum hourly rate just to walk in your door, and typical residential plumbing bids for a small house can average more than $4,000. This means that if you are willing to take the time and learn the plumbing trade it is well worth the effort. I have known many people who learned how to become plumbers, including a 75-year-old grandmother.

The hardest thing about plumbing is determining the size and location of the pipes. The first step in rough plumbing is to figure out what types of plumbing materials you will need and where they will go. Unfortunately, building plans do not normally include the location of pipes, only the location of the installed plumbing fixtures. All you will see on a set of plans are the locations of the sinks, toilets, and other plumbing appliances. This means that plumbing a house involves developing additional information that will help you locate all the important water supplies, waste pipes, and vent lines. Start with a copy of your local plumbing codes. This document will tell you all the important legal requirements of a plumbing system from pipe sizes to approved connections to venting requirements. If you follow these directions carefully, your plumbing inspection will be a snap.

Start by taking a set of unmarked home plans and drawing where the piping goes clearly on your plans. This involves a little bit of guesswork, but do not feel too bad because a plumber would have to do exactly the same thing. Lay out the supply line that brings the water into your home from its source outside the house to where it enters. Then, diagram how the water lines distribute the water to the various parts of your home. The important connection is the one made to the hot water heater, where cold water will be heated and run throughout the house as the hot water supply lines. Show the location of all the supply lines, cold and hot water lines, and waste pipe lines. If you need help, any plumbing supply house can provide assistance with the design. Some might even do it for you if you paid them a small fee and promised to buy your materials from them.

When all your supply lines are diagramed, diagram where your plumbing vents will go. Each plumbing fixture that has a waste line such as a toilet, a shower, or a sink will require a vent to the roof. Vent lines allow waste liquids to drain down the waste lines efficiently. When diagramming these lines, you can even color code the lines to make your drawing clearer. Use red for hot water lines and blue for cold water lines. Use green for waste lines and brown for vent piping. You will also need to size each pipe line — you can code these sizes into your diagram. The size of the piping will depend on your local plumbing codes. Water supply lines will be larger at the start and taper down. Waste and vent piping sizes will depend on distances. The building department or your local hardware store can help you size all the pipes.

This diagramming is the same step that most plumbing estimates make when they bid your plumbing work. It allows them to calculate how much piping they will need and how much labor it will take to set it. They measure all the plumbing lines and add the materials together to get a material estimate and then plug in a unit price for every foot of pipe to set for the labor. After this all they have to do is add a unit price for the labor to set each plumbing fixture. This might mean $175 for every toilet or $280 for every shower roughed in. This unit price is based on the plumber's past experience and how many labor hours it takes to actually set a fixture. Then your plumber will mark-up the bid and submit it to you to do the work. These unit price numbers are often the ones in the means unit pricing book previously mentioned.

If you are doing the work yourself, you do not need to be too concerned with the labor numbers. You can get a fairly simple idea of how much labor will be required by using averages. According to industry averages, a typical 2,500-square-foot house can be plumbed by two men in less than two weeks. Use this average to figure about how much time you will need.

The more important thing to the owner or builder is what materials you will need. After you have all of your plumbing diagramed, do a complete material take-off or have the hardware store do one for you. Again, the local hardware store or plumbing supply company can be useful in helping to size, supply, and drain lines and plumb your house to meet local building codes. Most of the information needed to properly plumb a house must be learned from a good source on plumbing. Plumbing codes are very specific about the size of drain lines, how far they can travel, how they are fastened, how they must be vented, and what types of connections are acceptable.

Because of the nature of an underground home, you may need to run your plumbing lines under or through the floor. Drain lines will probably also run through the floor. This means that some rough plumbing might have to occur as soon as you begin to prepare for your floor slab pour.

Waste pipe plumbing vents often must penetrate the roof structure. This means that vent piping needs to run through interior partition walls or be pre-installed in the foundation wall. Any roof penetrations must be properly sealed or they will provide an opportunity for water infiltration later. In conventional roof plumbing, the waste vents usually have the advantage of being installed on a steeply sloped surface. In earth-sheltered homes, the roof slopes can be much shallower, so penetrations must be more watertight.

Another important consideration with underground homes is to make sure that adequate floor drains are installed. These will function in the event of an emergency to catch any water that would normally cause flooding. These drain lines can be installed in the floor system with backflow prevention systems. Any plumbing leaks will then be dealt with by the floor drain system before they can cause flooding.

There is a wide range of materials available for plumbing in modern residences. Fifty years ago, the only options for water pipe plumbing were copper piping for supply lines and cast iron pipe for drain lines. Now, most residences use plastic supply lines and plastic PVC and ABS drain lines. Take the time to research all options that are available to you for the use of plumbing materials. Some piping systems are rigid and some have flexible piping that can be easily be run through internal walls or embedded in concrete. Be careful to steer clear of plastic materials that have been shown to cause leak problems in the past. Some types of plastic plumbing supply lines have been known to have problems when their connections fail and cause flooding in a residence.

Rough plumbing includes installing all water, waste, and vent piping before the walls are covered. Additionally, large shower or bath stalls may need to be installed while the house is still open because they will not fit through a regular doorway frame

Finished plumbing

Finished plumbing in earth-sheltered homes is also very similar to that in conventional homes. The differences, if any, lie in the septic or wood heat systems, or in systems designed to handle the recycling of water. Because underground homes are more susceptible to flooding, it is important to include several safety features in your finished plumbing. One is a catch basin below the hot water heater. This will catch any overflows of water from a broken hot water heater. It is also important to have the same type of catch tray under the clothes washer to prevent any problems from leakage of a water supply line. These types of catch trays are an inexpensive insurance.

Finished plumbing includes the installation of toilets, sinks, faucets, and hot water heaters. It usually occurs in the later stages of the home construction process after the walls have been covered. Installing these fixtures is very easy for anyone mechanically inclined and most plumbing bids break out rough and finished plumbing. If your bid does not, ask your plumber to do this. That way you have the option of doing this easy work yourself, even if you do not want to do the harder rough plumbing.

Saving money on plumbing work

One of the best ways to save money with plumbing is to insulate the hot water supply lines. Hot water supply lines radiate their heat and lose it to the environment. Insulation can conserve this heat and keep it from being lost. Hot water heaters are one of the largest electrical energy users in a home. Insulation blankets on the hot water heater are absolutely essential. The larger the hot water heater, the more energy it uses. Size your hot water heater so that it will provide for only your hot water needs. A 50-gallon hot water heater would be sufficient for a small two-person home. The 80- or 90-gallon tank should only be used in a larger family. They are sufficient for a four-member family. Some larger custom homes specify a loop system for continuously circulating hot water through the hot water pipe system in the home. This type of system will keep you from waiting for hot water when you take a shower and the shower is a long distance from the water heater. Such systems are a wonderful convenience but extremely expensive and a great energy water.

One recent cost-saving alternative to conventional hot water heaters that makes much sense is an on-demand or tankless hot water heater. On-demand water heaters work by heating water only when it is necessary and they do not keep a continuous supply of water hot all the time. When on-demand water heaters were first introduced in Europe after the Second World War they were costly and inefficient. Frankly, when they first came out, they just did not produce enough water quickly enough for showering or bathing and the hot water that they did produce was never sufficiently supplied to meet the demands of a hot shower or appliance.

Recent improvements in the technology of on-demand water heaters have made them much better. Many of the homes in Europe use these on-demand hot water systems very effectively. They are still more expensive to install than a regular hot water heater but quickly make up for their expense in the energy savings. Tankless or on-demand heaters can produce about two gallons of hot water a minute. Instead of storing the hot water all the time, this water is immediately used before it can even cool down. A traditional hot water heater can cost up to about $1,000 to buy and install, but is generally a bit less. A tankless system may run up to three or four times that cost, but the payback in energy savings can make up the difference in several years.

Other alternate hot water heaters can also save a significant amount of money. These include solar heating systems, wood heating systems, and gas water heaters. The roof solar water-heating systems can keep a continuous supply of hot water on hand for domestic use and also partially heat a home. They are best used in areas with high all seasonal sunlight. Large storage tubes on the roof of a residence can heat hot water in the daytime. This hot water can be pumped into insulated storage or circulated throughout the house to provide heat. People who have solar water-heating systems are always surprised by the amount of hot water that is produced. Many off grid homes use solar water heating systems for all their hot water needs.

Hearths or wood burning stoves with water heating systems can also be very efficient. A water heating hearth or stove is specially designed to have pipes running through parts of it, which can heat the water when the stove is operating. Instead of the electric coils in a hot water heater, the fire in the stove or hearth provides the energy to heat the water. If your primary source of heat is a wood stove, this may be a great system for you; if not you will have to have some type of backup water heating system.

Less exotic hot water heating systems include natural gas or propane hot water heater systems. These are extremely efficient and save electrical energy. Gas water heaters can be a very affordable option in areas of the county that have cheap gas readily available.

Some modern earth shelters go to the extreme of recycling water, purifying rainwater, or extracting water from saltwater sources. All of these systems provide interesting alternatives for off-grid living. Recycling water systems can use the same water source over and over again, especially for non-potable water. A very small supply of water can be used for showering, washing dishes, and watering the garden. Rain barrel collection systems are excellent for washing a car and keeping a vegetable garden well watered. In some areas where a resident is close to ocean water, reverse osmosis can be use to make saltwater pure. This, however, is still an expensive process.

Rain barrel collection systems, underground cisterns, low or no-flow toilets, and low-water-use appliances can also be used to conserve water resources. On-site wells can provide a less expensive non-utility source of water.

Septic systems can also rely on alternate technologies, although some building codes may mandate the installation of a regular drain field system. No-flow toilets require no water. They work by desiccating liquid and solid waste products. The other advantage no-flow toilets have is that they do not have a noisy flush that can wake people during the night. Some alternate septic systems also involve dehydrating solid septic waste and collecting it as dry compost for gardening.

In some cases, poorly drained lots require more extensive septic drainage systems. Many of these systems involve pumping septic waste uphill and mounding the waste in a special drain field. These systems are traditionally very expensive and require a contractor with specialized knowledge. Because of this, one of the things to make sure when you are buying a lot is that the drain fields can be built without any problems. This can be established by doing a perk test to test the drainage on the property as previously discussed.

CASE STUDY: BIOHOMES

Edward B. Dilley, Sr., Founder, Owner, and CEO of Tilted Planet Produc-
tions
10965 P.O. Box
Zephyr Cove, NV 89448
www.biohome.net
tppbiohome@aol.com

Project BioHome has been an ongoing quest since 1992. It is a research and development project into a completely "closed housing system." The idea is that each home should power itself, and also grow its own food, scrub its air, and recycle its water. It is total off-grid living where the home sustains its owner. To have such a design requires a totally new building concept, one that includes a completely sealed and controlled environment inside the home. Because it is an aboveground cave, Bio-home technology is easily adaptable to underground living.

The current earth base station BioHome No. 1 is located in a remote, harsh environmental area in the high mountain desert of Nevada. This location is 5,000 feet above sea level. Temperature extremes range from 35 degrees below zero to 110 degrees in the shade. Wind speeds can exceed 100 miles per hour on windy days. This new home concept is not for everyone, as it involves a lifestyle that not everyone is used to; but, for the hardy and those wanting to be self-sufficient, it is a dream home. Biohomes are durable, long lasting, and easy to heat. They have an insulation factor of R-90, which is five to seven times that of a typical house exterior wall. Biohomes take no energy to cool and only a tiny amount of energy to heat. The steel geodesic dome structure is coated with 8 inches of polyurethane foam and is anchored to a 7-inch-thick concrete earth slab floor.

The plumbing system includes a solar toilet that uses no water, a 20-gal-lon recycling kitchen water and shower system, and a solar still for drink-ing water production. The electrical systems include solar and wind gen-eration energy systems. Heating is done by in-floor radiant hot water heated by the sun. I have no ongoing monthly utility bill. My biohome is coated with a weatherproof coating that will last more than 50 years.

Building permits? No problem. This is an area of the country where building permits are not required. My property taxes on 20 acres are $40 per year. Sound like science fiction? Well, my biohome was built for one-quarter the cost of a conventional home, and I think it is a better product. By not conforming to conventional thought, I have created a home that frees me of the financial burdens most homeowners are slaves to.

Sometimes I do feel like I am living in a sci-fi movie, but my home is dependable and gives me a real sense of security and belonging. My home is a natural and sustainable part of its environment. It takes care of me rather than me taking care of it. Living with nature in this way gives a new meaning to the old expression "home sweet home."

Heating Work

Heating or cooling a home always requires energy but this is an area where earth-sheltered homes really shine. Their extreme efficiency means that about 80 percent less energy is required. This energy can come from any source. Solar power, wood burning, coal, oil or gas, electricity, or even geothermal hot water can be used to heat a home. In prehistoric times man used fire; today the options are much more abundant.

Probably some of the most exciting changes in home construction and energy usage have come in the form of heating and cooling improvements. Existing heating systems have become more efficient, and alternate systems have been introduced that save natural resources. Technological advances have made almost every heating source more efficient but even more it has had a long list of alternate ways to heat a home.

Wood heat

Wood heat is the most common method of heating underground homes. It is efficient and fairly inexpensive but requires more manual labor than other methods. A cord (or pile of wood 4 feet by 4 feet by 8 feet) runs between $100 and $300, depending on what part of the country you are in. This price can be even cheaper if you have your own land and can get the wood for free. The amount of wood you burn in a winter depends on many factors, like the coldness of the winter or the type of wood and the efficiency of your home. Conventional homes can usually be heated on 3.5 to 4 cords of wood per winter, but remember earth-sheltered homes are much more efficient. Reports indicate that some earth-shelter homeowners can survive in a cold winter on less than a cord of stove wood. This would be about $200 per year to heat a small home.

The use of a wood stove or installed hearth that burns cordwood or wood pallets can be used as a small home's primary heating source. Statistics show that most earth-sheltered homes rely on wood heating systems either as their primary heat source or as a secondary, backup heating system. Improvements in the efficiency of wood burning stoves and hearths have been made in the last few years. This has made wood burning a more attractive option. Many homeowners have access to inexpensive cordwood and wood pallets. This is incredibly convenient if you live in a wooded area. Some areas of the country restrict the use of wood burning during certain times of the year to help relieve air pollution. Every year, the Northwest has about two to four weeks when burning wood is prohibited. Fortunately exceptions to this rule usually exist when wood-burning heating is the primary heating source.

Wood pellets

Another recently developed alternative to burning cordwood is using something called a wood pellet stove. Wood pellet stoves burn small pieces of compressed sawdust instead of cord wood. Wood pellets are small, compacted pieces of sawdust about the size of a typical pill capsule. They are manufactured by the many lumber mills by compressing scrap sawdust. Because of this, they are considered less expensive fuel to burn. They are also considered a more convenient way to store and load a wood-burning stove. Instead of having to chop, split, and carry heavy chunks of cordwood all you have to do is load packs of small pellets.

Wood pellets are usually sold in one-ton pallets of about 50 plastic bags for a full pellet. The price of a pallet is from $200 to $300. Several pallets can heat a normal home for a winter. Each bag weighs 40 pounds. Bags can be easily loaded into your stove. They can now be purchased at just about any lumber store and even delivered to your doorstep.

Usually, wood pellets are first loaded into a storage area in your stove by the bag. A small augur motor then feeds the pellets to a combustion chamber that can burn the pellets with almost no ash produced. On some stove models a thermostat can change the speed of the augur motor to keep a constant temperature. On efficient stoves, one bag of wood pellets can last almost a whole day because they provide many conveniences — if they are kept dry. Wet pellets tend to absorb water and swell to about twice their original size. They also loss their pellet shape and become worthless as a fuel. Even though they come in plastic bags, the bags are not totally waterproof and some homeowners have discovered a pile of wet exploded bags of sawdust where their wood pellets once were.

Still, wood pellet stoves are more efficient that cordwood stoves and certainly much more convenient. They produce much less ash than a cordwood stove and are probably cheaper to operate.

This has made them a very attractive option both as a primary and as a secondary source of heating.

Passive solar heating

Passive solar heat is another common method of heating earth-sheltered homes. In areas of the country where there are numerous clear weather days, it is an excellent way to heat a home, even if used as a secondary source. Passive solar heat is very efficient and involves three major components. The first is a southern exposure to take maximum benefit of the sun during all seasons of the year. The second is some form of thermal mass to collect solar heat and store it for slow release in the future. The third method involves disseminating the stored heat throughout the house when it is most needed.

Using solar heating as a primary heat source can be a bit complicated. It involves complex heat loss calculations to make sure the system works as effectively as possible. Solar heating is something that is best designed by someone who is a professional and has experience designing solar heating systems. Because the design of a home determines the constraints on the solar heating system, it is important to incorporate the solar heating design considerations at the earliest stage possible. Some architects specialize in the design of solar heated housing and can handle all the calculations that are a part of the design.

Passive solar heating systems typically involve a solar wall of windows that collects the sun's heat during the daylight hours in the house. This collected heat is stored by some form of large thermal mass that collects the heat and releases it slowly over time. This works the same way that the hot pavement of a road stores heat on a sunny summer day. Thermal masses can be anything from a masonry block wall to large tanks filled with stored water.

In the earth-bag design, the thermal mass is a back wall with earth-filled bags. These bags accumulate the sun's heat and release it slowly at night when it is needed. In an Earthship house, the thermal mass is formed by a back wall of recycled earth-filled tires. These black, earth-filled tires are an excellent way to collect and release solar heat. Once the heat is stored in a solar mass, it can be disseminated throughout the house by the use of a simple ventilation system. Inexpensive fans and ductwork can spread the collected heat throughout the entire residence. These fans can be run continuously or designed to run in a way that keeps the heat balanced throughout the house.

Both solar and wood heat systems are considered sustainable. Supplementary solar and wood heat can be efficiently disseminated to heat to the entire residence. Forced air movement, flooring piping, or radiant walls and ceiling piping are also options that can be considered.

Adding a convection heating system to wood or solar heat can illuminate one of the major problems with both systems: they are point source heating. Both wood stoves and passive solar heating produce heat in only one area of a house. To take full advantage of these heating methods as a primary source of heating, some efficient way of disseminating the heat must be in place.

Conventional heating

Just because you are building an earth-sheltered home does not mean you have to use an alternate heating method. Conventional heat sources can also be used. These include such things as oil heat, gas heat, heat pumps, and electrical heating. Your conventional heating system will probably be sized smaller than were it in a conventional home. Energy usage will also be greatly reduced.

Heat pumps, which pull heat out of the air or from the ground like a reverse refrigerator, are a good conventional option for heating a home. Heat pump exchangers also offer the advantage of being able to heat a residence in the winter and cool it in the summer. In areas with high daytime summer temperatures, this is important.

Conventional forced air systems that use oil, gas, or electric heating systems can also be used to heat earth-sheltered homes. Remember, you do not have to rely on only one source of heating system. A residence that has wood heat can also have a backup baseboard electric heat system or a residence that relies primarily on solar heating systems can use oil heat as a backup.

One of the biggest practical problems faced by earth shelter builders is how to distribute heat effectively throughout the house. The predominate use of concrete floors, walls, and ceilings sometimes limits where ductwork can be installed. One popular method of heat distribution is to provide radiant hot water piping through the concrete floor slab or in the roof slab. Here, piping filled with circulating hot water is pumped from a central heating source to all areas of the home.

Another interesting way to disseminate heat in an underground home is to provide open areas above interior walls for the heat to flow naturally to every room. This passive flow system allows one central heat source, like a wood stove, to heat a room and then have the heat travel to other rooms over the top of each interior wall.

Radiant heating

One of the most exciting new innovations to come along recently in heating involves the use of radiant heat. Radiant heating uses hot water pipes embedded in the floor or ceiling to radiate heat to the residents. This is similar to the old hot water radiator systems that many houses used more than 50 years ago. Modern radiant heating systems can be installed in the floor or ceiling, and they provide comfortable and efficient heat. Radiant piping is usually placed in the concrete of the floor slab in a back-and-forth pattern to increase the area of radiation. In floor radiant heating, warm water is pumped through the tubing and heats the concrete floor by radiating its heat into the thermal mass of the concrete. The warm floor then radiates its heat to the occupants of the home. Radiant heat is becoming a popular option even in conventional homes, but it requires some form of thermal mass to make it effective. The primary advantage is that it provides a comfortable type of heating. Rather than heating all of the air in a home, the heat radiates to anyone standing near the radiating source.

Another thing that is nice about radiant heating is that it allows a residence to be divided into zones. One zone of the house can be selectively heated over other zones. With this system, you can design a timed zonal heating system that will heat only the living room during the day and only the bedrooms at night. Radiant-heated homes are said to be some of the most comfortable homes to live in. Radiant heat provides uniform heat throughout the home and leaves the residence free of cold or warm spots. The primary disadvantage of radiant heat is that it is difficult to install and when systems fail, repairs can be costly. Pipes that are imbedded in the floor are more difficult to install and when they have problems they are more difficult to access and repair. This system is also more expensive than other types of heating.

The installation of radiant heat primarily involves placement of piping in the floor slab before it is poured. Radiant in-floor heating requires insulation to be placed under the entire floor to prevent radiant heat loss down through the earth. Radiant in-floor heating also makes in-floor plumbing more difficult. The location of primary lines of heat must be carefully located so they do not interfere with water supply or drain lines that travel under or through the floor.

Summary

The utilities of your home form the backbone of its construction. Properly done electrical wiring, plumbing, and heating are the things that are going to make your home more livable and more comfortable over the course of its life. Saving money on these critical elements can be done if you are careful to preserve the integrity of the utilities system. The utilities of an earth-sheltered home are not much difference than the utilities on a conventional home. Innovative technologies have made all home utilities more efficient and easier to install in every respect. Taking advantage of some of these technologies may involve more upfront costs, but these costs will certainly be recuperated later on in the life of the structure. Be careful to balance benefits, convenience, and cost. Every house is different and every owner or builder must make the important decisions about what type of system is best for him or her.

Chapter 7

Home is where the Earth is: Erecting an Earth-Sheltered Homes

> *"Home, the spot of earth supremely blest/*
> *A dearer, sweeter spot than all the rest"*
> — *Robert Montgomery*

Erecting an earth-sheltered home can be an exciting process. After the footing, foundation, and floor are poured and cured, the structure can then be erected. This part of the process goes fairly quickly. Framed houses sometimes seem to almost appear overnight. You can drive by one day and nothing is there; but, just like a mushroom, a house will appear the very next day.

The erection of a house is also exciting because that is when you see the full potential of what the house on the property can really be. You can stand in the partially completed shell of the house and start to imagine and get a sense of what that house will be like to live in when it is completed. For the owner or builder, nothing is more exciting than seeing what his or her new view will be or how much room the master bedroom will have. If changes are to be made, the erection phase of construction is the time to make them. Now you will have a much better, three-dimensional feel of what the house is going to be like.

Exterior Walls

Concrete casting is usually used for the footing, foundation, and floor slab. Although footings are almost universally constructed of reinforced concrete, exterior walls that are in contact with the earth can be constructed of poured concrete, masonry materials, earth bags, earth-filled tires, or other alternate materials. Treated wood is also an option but usually discouraged. Walls in contact with dirt must have some form of treatment to protect them from earth contact. Earth contact can destroy untreated wood and has a corrosive effect on concrete and steel. Any earth walls must also be engineered to withstand the lateral loads of bermed earth. These lateral loads are much greater than anything a normal wood exterior wall would encounter. Earth bags and earth-filled tires can be stacked, with treatments applied to the earth-contact side prior to backfill. *The sides of an underground home exposed to the earth will require some form of water treatment, which will be discussed in Chapter 8.*

Wood Framing

Exterior walls that have no earth contact can be conventionally framed with wood lumber and siding, or they can be constructed with the same materials of which ground contact walls are made. Remember that any exposed wall will be visible and will need to be maintained just like the exterior walls of a conventional home. Because of this, it is wise to use durable materials and siding on exposed exterior walls. The use of masonry, or some long lasting material, is encouraged.

Typical wood framing on exposed exterior walls would include 2-foot by 4-foot or 2-foot by 6-foot stud walls with a plywood or foam board underlayment and some form of siding. This is often referred to as "stick" framing. Siding can be conventional wood siding, concrete lap siding, or alternate materials, such as stucco or brick. A large variety of exterior siding options exist, from vinyl siding to metal panel siding. One creative owner/builder decided to stucco the exterior wall with broken colored glass shards that had been rolled in a rock polisher.

Precast or Preformed Panels

Another option for exterior walls is to use preformed or precast concrete or polystyrene panels. One company that a friend of mine works with is currently building homes in Mexico using pre-formed polystyrene (plastic foam like Styrofoam) panels glued together and coated on the interior and exterior with an epoxy concrete. Styrofoam, once thought to be an environmental hazard because of disposal problems, has now been seen to be a great way to help save the environment. Recycled foam

Photos courtesy of Sustainable Green Building Corporation

can be used as the construction material, and because plastic foam has such a high R value, it is an amazing insulator. Polystyrene walls are structurally sound and walls and roofing systems can be constructed from it extremely rapidly. Using just a few simple tools and some glue, a full-size home can be erected in less than a week. Utilities like electrical and plumbing lines can be dug into the panels in little trenches and covered over with spray polyurethane foam. The polystyrene panels can be covered on the inside and outside with epoxy concrete. This material is fire resistant and saves having to cover interior walls with drywall or exterior walls with siding. Full home installations only need four or five different trades to completely erect a house.

The rapid construction aspect of this system also makes it extremely attractive as replacement housing after disaster relief. Palleted prefab homes can be delivered to an area and the whole superstructure can be erected in less than one week to provide emergency shelter. Because they are constructed of polystyrene, these panel homes might even be used in areas of hurricane reconstruction building, like Louisiana and Mississippi after Hurricane Katrina.

Several other companies manufacture precast concrete panel walls and roofs that can be rapidly erected. Many companies even offer modular prefabricated wall systems that can be set in place with a crane. Formworks Building Inc., the company featured in a previous Case Study in Chapter 3, will ship these panels to any area of the country for erection. The prefab panels have detailed instructions on how to put them together and can be erected very rapidly with unskilled labor.

The advantage of these systems is that they save significant amounts of erection time and expense. Although pre-manufactured materials are more expensive than site manufactured materials, they save money in the erection process by being installed much more quickly. This is especially true in places of extreme weather or where lot access is more difficult. In Southeast Alaska, precast concrete panels are commonly used. Here prefab fishing and hunting cabins can be manufactured in warmer areas and flown in by helicopter to remote camping areas. If you are considering using precast or preformed materials, get a firm bid on the erected product that can be compared to on-site forming of same design. Compare the costs carefully — you will be surprised.

Framing

Framing the interior of an earth-sheltered home can be much like framing the interior of a conventional home. Framing with two-by-four wood or metal studs is common. Because of their nature most earth-sheltered homes are one story, but second story floor framing can be accomplished very effectively with conventional wood floor framing. Interior framing should include provisions for running utilities and some form of wall treatment, like drywall or wood paneling. Exterior walls that are exposed concrete can be furred out with strips of wood and finished with drywall or paneling, or they can be left in their natural state. These walls can be textured and painted or left unpainted for a natural concrete appearance.

Building the roof

Roof structures on underground homes can be wood framed on bermed construction or underground construction. Conventional roof framing is usually inadequate to hold the required weight loads of an earth cover so heavy post and beam framing is usually used to carry the loads. This method of construction is also commonly known as timber framing. True heavy timber framing requires different framing skills than general carpenters are familiar with. Doing this type of work on a highly technical scale requires very skilled craftsman and may be more than the average owner or builder will want to take on.

The timber framing of Rob and Jaki Roy's famous Earthwood home was done on a simpler level, which required less skill and still provided a strong, economical superstructure that was fairly easy to construct. With simple posts and beams, they were able to construct a round support structure that could support about 60,000 pounds. Eight-inch posts supported a plank and beam ceiling structure that was then water-proofed for protection from the elements. The details of how they constructed this system are included in their book, which is listed in the reference section at the end of this book. Wood beams and plank ceilings appeal to many people because of the aesthetics of using wood.

Rather than working with wood, some people choose to work with more durable materials for the roof structure. Roofs on in-ground homes can be constructed of poured or precast concrete, structural steel, or even more exotic materials.

Pouring concrete on a roof structure also requires a high degree of skill, as previously discussed, and is not an option that should be attempted by the amateur or first-time builder. Precast panels are a different option, however. Precast panels can be ordered and installed conveniently from many concrete pre-casters. These companies can be found in most areas of the country or the product can be shipped in to the area in which you are building your home. Some of these precast concrete companies even specialize in underground home designs.

Though pouring roof structures is probably beyond the capability of most owners and builders, precast panels offer an attractive alternative to pouring your concrete roof. These panels are poured at a central manufacturing facility with high quality control. Precast panels are usually erected with the use of a crane and can be secured using a variety of different methods. They can be cast into the walls, secured with bolts, or post-tensioned. With post-tensioning, steel cables or metal rods are run through the panels, which are then tightened together. Grout fill is later pumped into the channels and hardens to form a continuous connection column. If you are interested in using precast panels, there is plenty of help available. Most concrete manufacturing plants have the capacity to manufacture precast panels. Several companies, like Formworks Building, Inc., will design, ship, and even help install panels anywhere in the United States or Canada.

The use of light-weight concrete alternatives, like shotcrete, is also an interesting option. These prefabbed sections are much lighter than a full reinforced concrete structure. Because of this, parts can be assembled more rapidly and are cheaper to produce. These structures can be produced as free spanning dome structures that give the homeowner more space without the restricting support posts. Clear spans without support posts give a room a much more open feeling of luxury.

Building Your Roof with Steel

Steel roof structures are also an option for your underground roof structure. Heavy steel beams can be bolted or welded together and supported with steel posts to provide a superstructure than can be covered with steel sheeting, wood planking, concrete panels, or poured concrete.

Steel has the advantage of being extremely strong for its unit weight and will support earth loads well. It is fairly easy to work with and can be an extremely flexible building system. Because of steel's good strength-to-weight ratio many modern commercial buildings structures, including high rises, are constructed out of steel. Because of this, steel is the primary building material in high-rise buildings.

The chief disadvantage is that steel is a more expensive material than other building materials. A steel beam used to span an open area might be three to ten times more expensive than its counterpart in wood. Combining steel with other materials like wood and concrete can help to defer some of this expense and in some cases steel beams can actually be cheaper than wood or glulam beams for long spans. A glulam beam is a composite beam made up of smaller pieces of wood glued together to create a larger beam. For larger wood beams, glulam construction is much less expensive that milling a beam out of solid wood. In some cases, it may even be impossible to even find a beam as large as some glulam beams for certain applications. Glulam beams can also be engineered for structural loads like steel beams.

Exotic Roofs

Many more exotic types of roof structures are also an option that can be considered. In this book, we will not go into great detail about these options because they are very extensive. In fact, a detailed inventory of these alternate building methods and how they are used would probably significantly influence the size of this book. Suffice it to say there are many other options available for roof construction, and many may be worth considering. All have advantages and disadvantages that need to be considered carefully. Some of these more exotic materials are still in the development stage. If you are interested in them there are many resources to explore. This section provides just a glimpse of some of the options you have.

Earth bags can be corbeled or laid with a slight offset to create small-domed structures. Roof domes can even be constructed from steel reinforcing bars and coated with urethane, fiber-reinforced concrete, or even more exotic materials. Pit homes can be constructed using wood logs and planking in a tepee support. Compacted earth can be corbelled or offset, stacked like earth bags to create a domed structure. Masonry roof structures can also be constructed from block, brick, or stone.

Perhaps one of the most creative options uses steel shipping transport containers that are podded together to create an underground structure. One creative architect even turned this idea upside down and created an in ground swimming pool out of a

10-foot by 10-foot by 40-foot steel container and a pool liner. He even built a deck around the edges for lying out in the sun and made provisions for solar heating of the pool water.

The point is that many creative options exist and your home may be enhanced by considering some of them. Some people are more comfortable exploring alternate building technologies than others. Usually, these options can offer some practical advantage, whether it be aesthetic or monetary. Some brave pioneers will always be exploring the boundaries of building construction, much like underground homebuilder Mike Oehler, who currently offers a book on low-priced underground home construction.

Covered roof structures in underground homes usually have much shallower pitches or slopes than those of conventional houses. This means that the roof is actually flatter and has less of a slope for water to run off. With a flatter roof less material is necessary for the roof structure and these materials are more efficiently used. Flatter-pitched roofs are less expensive to build because they use fewer materials, but as those in the rainy Northwest have learned, these roofs are also harder to waterproof. The flatter the roof, the easier it is for water to pond and leak through the roof. Keeping the roof steeper will make water run off more effectively.

If you find yourself building in an area that has heavy rain, try and keep your roof pitch at least at a level of one or two feet of drop for every 12 feet of run or greater. This means the roof drops one or two feet vertically for every 12 feet that you travel horizontally. This is called a $1/12$ or a $2/12$ pitch roof. The use of domed or arched roofs can solve the roof pitch problem and also give interior spaces a roomier feel. Unfortunately they can also add more complexity and expense to the design.

Designing your roof structure

How you lay out your roof structure will determine the comfort of the entire home. Newer homes sometimes add one or two feet to the standard eight-foot ceiling height to give a roomier feel to the home. Nine-foot ceilings feel much roomier than you would think an added extra foot to the ceiling height could provide.

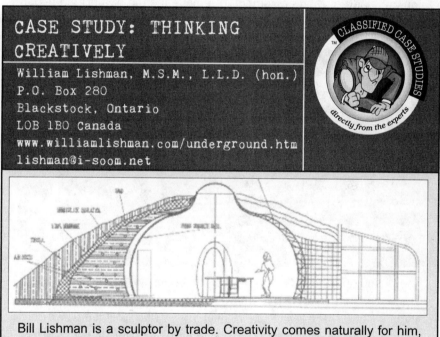

CASE STUDY: THINKING CREATIVELY

William Lishman, M.S.M., L.L.D. (hon.)
P.O. Box 280
Blackstock, Ontario
LOB 1B0 Canada
www.williamlishman.com/underground.htm
lishman@i-soom.net

Bill Lishman is a sculptor by trade. Creativity comes naturally for him, as his artistic pursuits range from writing to filmmaking and his personal interests include being an accomplished airplane pilot, inventor, naturalist, and entrepreneur. One of his art pieces, a 86-foot sculpture for expo '86, is featured in Vancouver, British Columbia. Several of his films have won distinguishing awards. Bill's autobiography has been published by Crown books and was made into a feature film *Fly Away Home*, released by Columbia Pictures Corporation in 1996. You may remember this film about a family of orphaned geese led home by a 14-year-old kid.

Lishman's first creative ideas for building underground came after constructing igloos in the snow one winter. He was amazed by how well it could be heated just by body heat alone. The property he was going to build on the top of a hill was very exposed to the wind and the protective aspects of underground construction had a strong appeal. Building square earth-shelters did not make sense to him however — square structures seem to inhibit the human spirit. So, inspired by British artist and designer Roger Dean, the idea of underground prefabbed domed structures was born in Lishman's mind.

His house on Purple Hill was designed as a series of interconnected underground dome igloos. Hiring family members to help in the construction and earth moving equipment to remove the top of a hill, he began construction on his home in 1988.

These domes have a central skylight that allows light into each room. The domes are constructed of $^3/_8$-inch mild steel rod grid embedded in about 3 inches of concrete, the domes are covered with sand and polystyrene foam, and EPDM membrane, and finally about 12 inches of topsoil to support a living roof. The inside surfaces were coated with white concrete marble dust mix for a bright white interior finish. An interesting detail used in the dome construction was a vertical steel central pole made of 2-inch black pipe that Bill used as a temporary brace during the construction process. This pole was moved from dome to dome as the residence was built because they only had one of them.

The doors and windows of Lishman's residence were torch cut out from the steel framework and custom fabricated prior to finishing. He used prefabricated, bullet-shaped gothic arched door frames. Finished amenities include conventional electrical wiring and plumbing with warm water radiant in-floor heating. Ventilation air is circulated from the  outside passively through air scoops and runs through a heat exchange system to recover warmth.

Lishman has come a long way since building his first earth-sheltered home. His latest ventures include helping others with the creative challenges of building earth shelters. For those interested in building with the system, he is certainly willing help. His open offer to act as a design consultant is backed up with an open invitation to personally visit his home (with an overnight stay if you like) and attend a detailed seminars on building the house design at a set cost. You are free to contact him for the details.

According to Lishman, constructing his dome house was a labor of love. Even after 20 years in the home, he loves to see how it awakens the child in anyone who visits. When asked about his design he says that just about anyone can build one but to remember that even though costs can be recovered over time this system cost more than conventional construction. A new prefab fiberglass module  system of similar design may bring the price down to compete with conventional construction techniques.

After reading Bill's literature, the biggest impression was that he is an artistic and creative force in earth-sheltered construction. The motto from his film — "to achieve the incredible you have to attempt the impossible" — seems very apropos when it comes to this creative man's visions and accomplishments.

Saving Money During the Erection Process

Proper planning is the best way to save money during the erection phase of your earth-sheltered home. This process will involve a large expenditure of labor and equipment resources. Effectively coordinating these resources can make an underground home more affordable. If heavy equipment is necessary, it should be coordinated so that the equipment is on site and uses as minimal an amount of time as possible. Construction cranes can run up to $300 an hour, and saving only a few hours through smart logistics can save thousands of dollars. Highly directed labor resources are also much more efficient than taking an unprepared approach.

Likewise, workers who do not know what they are supposed to be doing on a job site are far less efficient than workers who know exactly what to do. Make sure when you are paying workers your hard earned money that they are working productively by being organized and always having more work ready to assign to them.

Unavailable materials can also make your labor force inefficient and, consequently, more expensive. A worker who runs out of studs in the middle of framing a wall must run to the lumberyard to get more materials, which is much less efficient and more expensive than a framer who has all necessary materials and has no down time. Nothing hurts a large project more than not having the essential materials and equipment available when they are needed. Constantly running to the lumberyard for miscellaneous materials, tools, and equipment easily can easily triple the cost of any construction project.

How planning can help you save

One of my local builder friends said that the first house he built took him six months and $185,000 dollars to build. Four years later, he can build the same home design in three months for $20,000 less. When I asked him what the big difference was, he told me what he had learned was that all he had to do was to keep his lead worker from having to run to the lumber store every day to pick up missing materials and he would save a huge expense and plenty of time. By having all the materials onsite and ready to go, he avoided the lost time of having a productive worker run last minute errands, saved the expense of running to the lumber yard, and avoided the inevitable waiting that took place by an otherwise productive crew. Still, I believe many new homebuilders learn this lesson the hard way.

Picking Out Your Tools in Advance

Having the correct tools available can also save you money. A carpenter using the proper tools is much more productive than one who uses tools that are not appropriate. As the expression goes, "for want of a nail ... the kingdom was lost," and for want of a tool, many projects have been come to ruin. For example, cutting lumber with an inexpensive power handsaw is much slower than using a full power one. A good saw can cost another $50 to purchase, but save its cost in several days worth of work.

Inexpensive tool outlets offer fairly good quality hand tools for 20 to 40 percent less than the mainstream hardware stores. In fact, be careful buying anything at these stores. They usually offer great convenience, but the prices can be much more expensive than planning and selecting your sources carefully. One carpenter friend of mine buys all of his tools online, using auction sites like eBay. He has saved thousand of dollars over the years because of this. When you do buy materials or tools from a full-service hardware store, make sure you have them bid on a package of materials and negotiate the best price. Some stores will offer up to a 20 percent discount for the first purchase of materials made after an account is open.

The equipment necessary for the erection of an underground home can be quite varied and ultimately depends on what type of construction you are doing. If you are stacking earth bags, all that may be necessary are a few good shovels and a wood frame on which to set the plastic bags, but if you are erecting a post-tension precast panel wall, you may need a crane, concrete jacks, and spreading bars. If you are installing post-tension panels, you may need special cable tensioning equipment, as well as grout pumps. Each type of installation requires different types of equipment. Being prepared with the proper equipment is important in every case.

Concrete precast panels may weigh thousands of pounds. A crane will be necessary to lift these panels into place. Post-tensioning cables might need special jacking equipment to be jacked into place. These are used to tie the panels together and usually require a higher level of expertise than simple cast-in-place concrete. Expensive mortar injection pumps might be necessary to inject the mortar fill around post-tension cables. As discussed, finding the appropriate equipment involves thinking ahead about the construction process and planning for it properly. Most of this type of equipment is rentable at a local rental store but sometimes you will need to call ahead to reserve and find out what is available.

The Art of Negotiating

Unfortunately this book does not have a chapter on negotiation, but negotiating good prices on your construction materials is a very important part of saving money. To negotiate properly, you always start by clearly defining exactly what you want. If this includes material packages, make sure that the package you are bidding on is as clearly defined as possible and that you have a firm number to start your negotiations from. A typical building package for the lumber framing might include all the lumber necessary to frame the exteriors walls, any floor framing materials, and the roof structure. Remember, the terms of the deal are also very important. If you get a good price try to add on a free delivery, and see what the supplier says.

If you are negotiating with the subcontractor, the key is to clearly define every part of the work before you negotiate price. If you do not, you will always have left a back door for the subcontractor to renegotiate his bid. For example, one of the best negotiators I ever knew spent every day of his working career negotiating with subcontractors. On his full-time job, he negotiated large sized subcontracts worth many millions of dollars constructing commercial medical properties. He always started his negotiation by inviting the subcontractors to his office and grilling them for more than an hour about every detail contained in their bid, line item by line item. If the bid was for plumbing, he would go through every line item on the bid and verify the quality and type of every type of piping. He also educated himself a great deal on the type of work being done so he knew where the costs were. Once he had firmed up the final price and all of the particular details, he would begin to use the carrot and stick to entice a lower price out of the subcontractor. Once he had negotiated the best price, he would leave the room for several minutes and then return with a big smile, telling the subcontractor that he would like to do business with him, but can only manage to pay 95 percent of the price they had just negotiated. Please consider our offer carefully on your way home and call us tomorrow with a response. The implicit understanding was that if the subcontractor failed to say yes, he or she would lose the project. In actuality, even if the offer were turned down the next day, he would still offer to do business with the subcontractor. This strategy actually lowered the subcontractor's bid about half of the time, just by negotiating.

A gentleman I once did business with taught me a good deal about the fine art of negotiations. When I would give him a price on a project, his reaction was always to flinch and say "Wow, way too high." After hearing this response, the natural reaction of anyone would be to lower the price. I soon learned that this was a negotiation strategy he used with everyone he did business with. I verified this strategy one day by quoting him my cost on a project. Sure enough, I received the same shocked reaction when I gave him my price. I soon learned to start by giving him a higher price and waiting for his reaction and then negotiating a settlement. The trick here was to negotiate with him while he was negotiating with me.

Selecting your Materials from the Appropriate Places

Another area where significant savings can be made is in the selection and pricing of materials. Correctly sourcing and pricing materials is both an art and a science. Finding the right source for a product can make a huge difference in what you pay for it. This can take some time, but it is usually worth the investment. Remember not every product sources is equal. Some lumberyards even specialize in certain types of lumber. My favorite builder trick is bidding similar material packages to several sources and using the competition factor to drive the cost of the product down. On my last home lumber package, I was able to save $2,200 by having several suppliers bid against each other. In a tough economy each supplier wanted the job enough to give me his or her absolute lowest price. By having them compete against each other I was able to drive down the price I paid and save significant money.

Another product source often overlooked is second-hand sources. This includes recycled or used materials. Many second-hand building sources also exist. Although all used materials can offer some significant cost savings, be careful about purchasing used structural lumber. With used structural materials, you can sometimes run into building code restrictions. The problem lies in the strength of the wood beams and structural lumber used. New lumber that is produced in a lumber mill always carries a grade stamp. This stamp certifies the type and strength of the lumber. The following picture shows how grade stamps work.

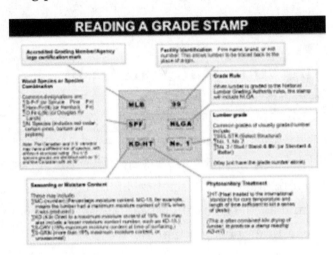

READING A GRADE STAMP

- Select Structural (Sel Str) No.1, 2, & 3

- Construction (CONST)

- Standard (STAND)

- Utility (Util)

The grade stamp specified where lumber comes from, what type of wood it is and how high of quality it is. Lumber is normally graded to utility grade, standard grade, construction grade, and three different grades of select structural grade. The grade of lumber tells the inspector what lumber can be used for. Some parts of a structure require structural lumber and some do not.

When lumber is used, it is ungraded and the strength of ungraded lumber cannot be easily determined. With ungraded lumber, the building inspector will have a very difficult time determining what grade of lumber it is because it does not carry the new lumber stamp. Consequently, used lumber is often prohibited in any area that has structural use. This includes posts, beams, or joists, which carry a specified design load.

This is not to say, however, that including used lumber for siding or interior wall covers is unacceptable. Flooring or other non-structural applications can also be done with used lumber when accepted by the code officials. Used lumber sometimes make a very attractive siding or interior wall covering — it jut can be used for the structural parts of your home. For example, the exposed wood ceiling in my kitchen is a beautiful cedar tongue and groove car decking, which is a type of lumber that interlocks and forms a beautiful pattern. This lumber was recycled from a school that was demolished in Eastern Washington more than 30 years ago. In its use in my home, it is non-structural.

Used doors, windows, light fixtures, and other non-structural components can also be easily incorporated into your home to give it that special touch of class. Old stained glass windows from churches and antique door fixtures are particularly popular. There are also many companies that supply used construction materials and specialize in selling used building materials. Old claw foot tubs, brass fittings, and plumbing fixtures are especially attractive. They can be used to really dress-up the finished plumbing of your home. Charity auctions, garage sales, and thrift stores also offer a great venue for finding used building materials. One local Rotary charity in our area has a yearly auction for everything from floor mold trim to door knobs and cabinet hardware. Including used materials can be a great way to save money, and it also has the potential to add a unique character to your home as well.

Finding the Right Equipment

Finding the correct equipment for every building task will also improve your work efficiency. Scaffolding is inexpensive to rent and makes working higher than five feet above the ground much more efficient for a construction crew. When used properly, power tools can also leverage construction labor. Ripping plywood panels may be done much more quickly on a table saw than with the use of a hand skill saw. Sometimes finding the appropriate equipment involves educating yourself on what the best equipment might be. Special routers, drills, and milling tools can be found to make almost any job easier.

One of the most exciting technological improvements to the construction process has been the introduction of cordless tools. Air-powered nail and screw guns can immensely improve the productivity of a carpenter. A carpenter with an air nailer can literally place more than ten times the number of nails in the same period of time as a carpenter using a basic hammer. Cordless sawzalls (reciprocating saws), drill motors, finishing saws, and even cordless chain saws can make construction go more smoothly. Many hardware stores even have cordless CD players and radios available to provide job site entertainment, as well as cordless vacuum cleaners to clean up a job site at the end of the day.

Photo courtesy of Earth Shelter Technologies, Inc.

Sweat equity

One of the most powerful ways to save money on your home is by using your own labor. Any savings on a construction project by the use of owner labor is called sweat equity. Using your own labor may not, however, mean doing every task yourself. Smart sweat equity involves using your labor in the most practical and efficient way possible. If a project requires three people to erect a retaining wall, take the most productive workstation. This may not be the job of actually erecting the wall or excavating for the wall, but supplying materials to the wall builder. The material supplier can determine the pace of construction, making the other two work partners more efficient in the process. In this position, he or she can also oversee the construction process and supervise the quality of work.

To get an idea of how powerful sweat equity can be, imagine that the average home takes from 2,000 to 6,000 labor hours to construct. At the time of this book's writing, the average labor rate for a construction worker hovers between $18 and $30 an hour. Your rate will depend on the area that you are in and the skill level of the worker. Based on these numbers, owners/builders using their own labor can save from $30,000 to $100,000 on a home construction project. These kinds of savings cannot be found in any other way.

Building Problems

In a perfect world, every construction project would take place in a warm, sunny day and everything would always go smoothly. Unfortunately, it is not always a perfect world — Murphy's Law also applies to construction projects. What can go wrong some-times does go wrong and being prepared for the challenges of construction can be very exciting. In earth-sheltered construc-tion, like any type of construction, what can go wrong sometimes does, and even the best-organized project can sometimes turn into a small nightmare. Dealing with problems effectively on a construction site is another way to save money on your project.

Scheduling problems

The types of problems homebuilders face on a day-to-day basis primarily involves scheduling. On construction projects, 60 per-cent of all complaints revolve around time and the performance problems associated with it. Construction scheduling usually involves critical paths that are determined by the delivery of materials and tasks performed by subcontractors. These paths are critical because other tasks depend on them and cannot get done without first being done. One good example is doing the rough electrical. Rough electrical cannot be done until the house is dried-in or protected from the elements. If you have a roofer scheduled for a Friday and he calls on Wednesday and says he will be a week late that means all other functions are also now postponed a week including the electrical work.

When these critical tasks and materials are delayed or a subcon-tractor does not perform promptly huge problems can result. Be-cause of this, most construction management involves identify-ing and managing the critical paths.

As you have learned from this chapter so far, having the proper materials at the right time can save you money on a construction project. Not having these materials can lead to all sorts of problems. One critical phase of home construction is something called the "dry-in." In order for a house to be "dried-in," the roof must be watertight. If critical materials, such as roofing or waterproofing materials, do not arrive on time, your whole project can be held up. Lack of waterproofing materials can keep other critical elements like plumbing, electrical, and interior finishes from being completed. This can ultimately cost you money and delay the whole project.

Always order materials ahead of schedule and allow plenty of time for delivery. Delays in getting materials delivered early can also cost money. If you discover at the last minute that you must have certain materials onsite by a certain date or it will hold up other tasks, you may end up having to pay more for the delivery fees on expedited delivery. A simple thing like a needing skylight flashing can hold up the whole roofing process.

A helpful tool when planning the schedule of construction of your home is laying out all key elements to make sure that they work smoothly together. Many builders use a scheduling program, like Microsoft Project, to monitor and manage the process of construction.

When subcontractors are delayed in their performance or perform poorly, the delays can also cause you problems and add extra expense. An electrical contractor who fails to complete the electrical rough on time can keep you from finishing the interior of your home. Delays can cost you extra finance fees, throw off other subcontractors, and keep you from moving in on time. Every builder's nightmare involves a subcontractor who, for some reason or another, shuts down a project by not performing on time. This can happen for many reasons. A subcontractor may be too busy to give your project the attention it deserves. The subcontractor might also not be qualified for scheduling the projects they have committed to. In any case, you must be prepared to deal with any subcontractors.

Avoiding problems

Schedule your subcontractors carefully and call them to remind them that you will need them. Let them know clearly that you have no tolerance for delays and you expect them to be onsite on time. If timing is really critical, with a questionable subcontractor it also helps to have a good contract that specifies monetary damages for failure to perform on time. Some commercial contracts even go so far as to specify something called liquidated damages for delays to the project. This is a set amount of money that the subcontractor will owe you for every day of delay. Some homeowners have even been known to back-bill subcontractors for job delay costs they felt were justified.

If all else fails, it helps to have a contingency plan. Be prepared to threaten to call or call another sub to fill in as soon as you see there is a severe problem. Make sure your contract also allows you the option of terminating your contract quickly and not being assessed any monetary penalty for unfinished work.

The key to preventing delays caused by critical elements of your project is identifying every key element and planning for it carefully. For example, if a subcontractor is scheduled on your project in a week, place a reminder call to remind him of your schedule. Place a follow-up if the subcontractor does not show up on time. Be sure to word any contracts with subcontractors carefully. Make sure that you have withheld enough money to assure timely completion of your project; this may include withholding enough money to hire another subcontractor if the one you have committed to flakes out.

Dealing with subcontractors

Subcontractors can also be a source of problems in other ways. Poor or negligent performance on a project has the potential to cause more damage than the value of a contract. But, good contracts can help assure proper performance on a project. Construction contracts are designed as a powerful tool in the industry. Most contractors and subcontractors are very familiar with contract law. Unfortunately, most industry contracts are one-sided against the customer. They are designed to protect the subcontractor in his or her day-to-day operations with many different customers. Standard contracts include provisions for creating powerful ways of protecting the subcontractor's interests.

Take the time to educate yourself about construction contract law because what you learn can save you money. Most states require contractors and subcontractors to post bonds for their work. If you have problems with a subcontractor, their security bond is insurance for you that the job is done properly. If you run into problems on your job caused by contractor negligence, you can actually attach a claim to the subcontractor's bond for any real damages. Most states also require subcontractors to provide release of liens on all work they have done before final a payment is made. It is important to get these signed releases before you completely pay off a subcontractor. Otherwise, you may be liable to pay for materials or labor that they have used on your job and not paid for. When a subcontractor goes out of business or does physical damage to your project there are very few legal remedies you can take. This is why it is important to check out all the subcontractors that you will be doing business with prior to starting your work. Subcontractors who have a good record of working with people will have a clean record with not only the Better Business Bureau and past customers, but also with your state.

Another important part of selecting good subcontractors is verifying with your state that they are properly licensed, insured, and bonded. Dealing with subcontractors who do not have these in place may seem like it can save you money, but it also cost you much more. Most states have very strict laws about dealing with unlicensed contractors. If you deal with an unlicensed contractor, your liability is very great. For example, Washington State requires all contractors be licensed, bonded, and insured for the specific type of work they do. If you deal with an unlicensed contractor or subcontractor, they have no legal recourse to collect funds from you for the work they do, but if they get injured on your job, you may be liable for their injuries. As the owner of the property, you may also be liable for any uncollected taxes they fail to pay the state and any subcontractor's they hire to do the work for them and fail to pay. What this means is that if you hire an unlicensed contractor to do your plumbing, you are not legally obligated to even pay them for their work. Any legal claims that the subcontractor may make against you for injuries on the job might be disqualified by your homeowners insurance and can become a direct liability to you personally. The way to ensure that this never happens is to verify the status of your contractor prior to doing business with them. Most states, like Washington, have websites which allow you to search for licensed contractors. Washington State's site is **https://fortress.wa.gov/lni/bbip/Search.aspx**. To check a contractor, all you have to do is type in the name of the company and it tells you its license number, insurance company, and bond information. Taking the time to do this can save you many headaches.

If you are hiring people to work under you as labor help, there are also legal requirements that must be met. State departments of labor and industry (L&I) insurance, unemployment taxes, and other state and federal taxes must be paid on any employee working for you. If you do not pay them, you may be liable at some future date for them plus penalties. This can be a very large liability. For example, a worker that you have paid $20,000 worth of wages to might owe an additional $3,500 of taxes and insurance to your state. If the person you hired for labor fails to pay these taxes, as the person's employer, you are obligated to pay the taxes with interest and penalties. Keeping track of this information can be a very time consuming process.

If you are using plenty of labor help, consider hiring your help from an employment service company. These companies will do all the bookkeeping for you for a fee. Any laborers you find and wish to use can usually be referred to the labor service company and hired out through them. Legal taxes will usually add about 20 to 30 percent to your base labor costs. Hiring labor through an employment service might add another 40 percent. The advantage of using labor services is that you only need to pay for labor when and where you need it. Thus, efficient management of temporary labor can save you significant amounts of money over keeping an employee continuously on payroll. A good example of this might be sending your labor home early if the weather is bad rather than keeping them on the payroll all day. Another example might be hiring five people for one day to help you with a concrete pour and letting them go the next day. This saves money because you are paying for labor only when you need it. Hiring people "under the table," or off the tax roles (even if they are your relatives), is a dangerous game.

Encountering Other Problems

KEY THINGS THAT CAN CAUSE PROBLEMS ON CONSTRUCTION PROJECTS
Loss of financing
Running out of funds
Unanticipated expense
Material delays (back-orders or shipment delays)
Incorrect or poor materials
Shortage of labor or labor poorly trained for task
Subcontractor not on time
Poor subcontractor work
Subcontractor errors
Construction errors (that will need to be corrected)
Late construction inspections
Weather delays

Shoddy workmanship

Other construction problems include work changes, incorrect construction, and shoddy workmanship. Incorrect construction can sometimes occur when blueprints were misread or incorrectly interpreted. Small notes on a blueprint can make big differences in how construction is executed. A framer who once worked for our company told the story about framing a whole house backwards. The key was a small note written on the bottom of the approved blueprints, which stated that this home was a reverse print. That means that every interior wall would be framed backwards from what the plan showed. He framed the house according to the print, which was backwards from the way the architect wanted it. Needless to say, the framer had to reframe the house correctly to get paid. In reframing the house correctly, he lost time and money — all the result of not carefully reading the blueprints.

Every mistake that is made on a construction project is said to cost five times its original cost. This is because something done wrong must be redone and while you were doing it wrong, you could have been doing it right. You could also have been doing something else while you were doing it wrong and while you were correcting it.

Shoddy workmanship can occur on a project any time the project is not consistently and effectively monitored or supervised, thus supervising subcontractors and contract labor requires consistent diligence. Just because a subcontractor has plumbed a house before does not mean that his or her workers are plumbing your house correctly. Keep a careful watch on any work that is being done, and do not release funds on completed work that does not meet with your complete approval. Also, keep a careful eye on the work being done by anyone under you. A day laborer assigned an important task can do plenty of damage in one day if he or she is not properly supervised.

Quality work comes from knowledge, practice, and experience. Most people run into problems on their first attempt at anything. If this is a new project for you, start by doing careful research and becoming knowledgeable about what you are doing. Take the time to practice and learn the skills necessary to be successful. Be patient and take the time to work carefully at the start. Most of all do not be afraid to make mistakes (learning always involves mistakes).

Knowing what can go wrong and how to deal with it can keep you from losing money. The most important part of building your home is to maintain a positive attitude. A positive attitude can make any problem seem smaller than it actually is. Do not let yourself get discouraged; every day is a new day.

Weather

One of the biggest construction problems that can really hinder progress is foul weather. Bad weather can make the simplest tasks harder to perform. Cold weather can keep concrete from curing properly. Extremely warm weather can drain even the hardiest worker of energy. Heavy rain can make working unpleasant and productivity can drop to nearly zero, and dealing with foul weather is a part of almost every construction project. Most earth-sheltered homes require at least four to eight months to construct (about the same time it takes to construct a conventional home), which means that the construction crew will probably have to deal with some extremes of summer or winter weather, or both.

The best way to deal with bad weather is to plan for it. Cold weather pours can be improved with the use of accelerants in the concrete or covering pours with blankets of hay. Starting a construction project earlier in the day can help you beat the heat, as it will help you avoid working during the hottest part of the afternoon. Heavy rains can be dealt with by using a flexible work schedule that allows the crew to stop working during the poorest weather.

Almost every construction project will have some weather-related problems to deal with, so decide your strategy for productivity early on. Warm weather productivity can be increased by making sure cold drinking water is available on site. Likewise, cold weather construction crews can be made more efficient when they are warmly dressed and have gloves. Crews working in heavy rains are much more productive when they are wearing the correct rain gear and boots.

One construction crew working in the winter of southeastern Alaska was able to deal with the cold weather despite the fact that it was dark almost all day. Because of the winter season, the sun never rose above the mountain horizon for 24 hours. The working day became perpetual dusk for them. Heavy-duty work lights allowed them to increase their efficiency and remain productive. On the flip side, they enjoyed almost 24 hours of daylight in the summertime.

Running over budget

Every construction project runs the risk of going over budget. The causes for this can be varied. When calculating construction costs, you learned that it is easy to miss important materials and to underestimate the labor necessary to complete a project. For this reason, every project should contain a contingency for cost overruns, but cost overruns are not always the result of just missing costs. The most severe cost overrun problems occur from unforeseen expenses.

Unforeseen expenses can add plenty of cost to your project. A contractor installing a footing in an underground home in Maine may be forced to spend additional money blasting stone ledge out of the way. This additional expense is passed to the owner in the contract as an unforeseen expense. The owner, not the contractor, ends up paying for unforeseen expenses. Because of its nature, avoiding unforeseen expense is very difficult. It is the major reason most large government contracts always over budget.

The best example of unforeseen expense can be seen on large government highway contracts. Public highway contracts are usually awarded to the lowest bidder. Unfortunately, it is very difficult to know the full extent of unforeseen expenses on a public contract. Most government bids try to plan for such expenses by getting unit price costs from the successful contractor for any contingency. If a highway project encounters low, water-filled land that needs to be removed and replaced with better fill material, the awarding agency will know how much it costs to remove this soil per yard and how much it costs to bring in new soil per yard. However, this does not keep them from having to spend more public funds.

For the private homebuilder, the same type of challenge can exist. Knowing your costs from your original budget and being prepared for the costs of any changes can be very helpful.

If while building you discover you need 300 more yards of fill, knowing the cost of this fill will allow you to negotiate better and perhaps find the best price for the additional materials. The key is to pay attention to the planning you have done, and to try to anticipate the things that can happen during a project. The best strategy is to plan for the best and be prepared for the worst. Fortunately, unforeseen expenses are not common in home construction projects and when they occur, they usually happen in certain categories. Subsurface conditions are a prime candidate. Subsurface conditions are the conditions hidden under the soil that affect building. In certain parts of the country, blasting rock ledges is a bigger hazard than other parts of the country. In other parts of the country, water problems may be a bigger risk. In Maine, for example, the subsurface conditions can be brutal. Glacial fields filled with silt can be underlain with hard rock ledges. These ledges are hidden from view and impossible to see until you start excavating. So if you live in Maine, you should be prepared for such hidden rock ledges and have a contingency plan in place in case you happen to discover one that needs to be blasted for your footing.

Changes to the project can also produce cost overruns. Almost every construction project has some changes. This is because 2-D plans rarely portray a 3-D world accurately and also because people will sometimes change their minds. As you are building you might discover that a window will look much better 2 feet to the left of where it is supposed to be installed. You might change your mind about the type of front door you want in your house after you see how unattractive the one you bought looks once it is installed. Do not be afraid of changes, but plan for them.

Most of the changes on your project should be covered in your construction fund. This is the set aside fund we discussed under estimating, which acts as a contingency to catch unforeseen expenses. If this fund becomes depleted, you always have the option to reduce or delay any construction changes. When you are doing the project yourself, you have the option to delay the completion of less critical items until a later date. Many elements of the finish work can be delayed without affecting the final sign-off on completion of the house. Then, you can come back later and finish these items.

Making Things Fit

Another big problem in home construction is making things fit. The average home has close to 10,000 different elements that must come together, and all of them must work for the home to function properly. When constructing your home, you may find something that does not fit. The door ordered for the front of your residence might be too big to fit into the framed opening. You may discover that the expensive final counter finish designed for your master bathroom is 3 inches too long, or that the custom cabinet ordered for the corner of your kitchen is ¾ inch too short. In home construction, these are common problems. Be prepared to deal with these types of problems with patience and good humor. Most of these problems can be addressed fairly simply: The door framing can be modified to fit the door, or a new door can be ordered. The custom cabinet that is too short can be filled with a cover panel. The expensive counter finish in the master bath, however, may have to be reordered, resulting in the loss of a few hundred dollars. Ultimately, that cost must be chalked up to educational expense. You will learn much about building this way.

One of my favorite homebuilding stories is about a builder who framed a roof structure with a large and expensive glulam beam that was custom cut and set in place. Rather than have the expense of a crane, he paid seven workers for six hours to help erect the beam and secure it in place. At the end of the day, to his great dismay, he became aware that the beam had been set at an incorrect roof pitch, even after measuring. The next week, when a new beam was ordered — at a cost of $800 — the same seven workers had to be re-hired to remove the beam and re-erect the new beam to the correct pitch. The wise carpenter's advice to measure twice and cut once should never be ignored.

Saving money by troubleshooting

The cost of construction problems can be reduced with proper troubleshooting. The art of troubleshooting is what makes home-building so attractive to some people. Some contractors thrive on being able to solve construction problems. Every task, from finding the right architect and the perfect subcontractors to sourcing and purchasing materials, can be seen as a challenge to solve. Even deciding when each phase of the project should be done can present challenges that need to be solved by the successful builder. Research helps, but experience is the greatest teacher.

Summary

Erecting any home is challenging, but building an earth-sheltered home involves even more challenges. Depending on the type of construction method used, building an underground home involves many talents and skills not the least of which is the ability to troubleshoot problems that arise during the construction process. Being prepared for these problems is the best strategy an owner/builder can take. Dealing with inclement weather, construction delays, and managing subcontractors can tax the energies and patience of any builder, but keeping a positive attitude through the process will keep the construction on track and on schedule.

The best words of advice are to seek out good counsel, maintain a good attitude, and avoid discouragement in all cases. Many owners and builders have found that building an earth-sheltered home is not only one of the most challenging endeavors, but also one of the most rewarding ones. Always be open to new ideas, and you will find creativity is the best way to add value to your home.

Chapter 8

Here Comes the Rain: Insulation, Waterproofing, and Ventilation

Some of the most unglamorous elements of construction include things that are hard to get excited about. These are things like waterproofing, insulation, and the mechanics of ventilating of your home. For most people it is very hard to get excited about fiberglass batt or hard board insulation let alone worrying about how to handle the humidity in your home. Just because they are not exciting, however, does not mean they are not important. In fact, waterproofing, insulation, and ventilation are probably the most important elements when it comes to the comfort of your home. In this chapter we will discuss these elements and how to see that they are done properly in an earth-sheltered home. This includes how to properly insulate, waterproof, and ventilate this type of home.

Properly insulating, waterproofing, and ventilating an underground home is considerably different than the same processes in a conventional home, and many of the differences are counter-intuitive. In earth-sheltered homes, these elements of construction are the most important ones to address properly if you wish to assure the maximum comfort and least amount of headaches later on. When they are done correctly, you will end up with the best of all worlds. When the processes are not done correctly, you can end up with a nightmare. Dancing in the rain may bring happiness, but so will a well insulated, waterproofed, and ventilated earth shelter.

Because the earth provides such a powerful heat sink, its stabilizing properties sometimes destabilize an underground home by actually sucking the heat away from the home. Insulation can be the best way of mitigating this problem. It provides a barrier that helps the earth stabilize and protect the temperature of your home. The proper placement of insulation can also keep your home from developing condensation problems. This is a big problem particularly in areas of the country with high humidity.

The proper waterproofing of an underground home is obviously exceedingly important in areas of high rainfall, but occasional torrents of rain need to be planned for in the desert, as well. More than one owner/builder has found himself or herself with a hillside lot that provides an almost continuous stream of water regardless of where he or she digs. These artesian wells are nice if you want water, but horrible if you do not. In some cases, they can even make a beautiful hillside view lot unbuildable for an earth shelter. Proper waterproofing includes suitable drainage, storm retention, and installation of water infiltration barriers all designed to keep the water on the outside of your home not on the inside. These must work the first time because second changes are extremely expensive.

Proper ventilation in an underground house will keep your home safe and comfortable. Good ventilation is one of the factors that can make an earth shelter much more livable than a regular home basement. It can keep the dank and cold feeling out and replace it with a warm, cozy, healthy airflow.

Waterproofing

If you talk with any earth-shelter homebuilder the first thing they will tell you is that the single most important aspect of underground home building is keeping the water out. Water finds its natural abode underground, which is why for centuries the best place to find water was to dig a hole in the ground or a well. But, water is not a good thing to have in your home. Infiltration of water can lead to mold, mildew, rot, and decay, and generally a miserable deterioration of a structure.

One of my good friends worked for an insurance repair contractor and was called in after broken water pipes created huge disasters in a residence. The failure of such pipes could result for many reasons but the end result was always the same. Water damage would create warped floors, crumbling sheetrock, and carpet rot. One story he tells is of a hot tub pipe that broke on the third floor of a house and did more than $50,000 worth of damage to the floors below.

The key then is to keep the water out and dry, comfortable conditions inside. As mentioned in previous chapters, water protection starts in the planning phase of construction with onsite drainage. Many jurisdictions require some type of drainage plan as a part of the building permit application, but some do not. It is up to the owner or builder to come up with a workable drainage plan. In any case, the first step is always to start with lot drainage.

Onsite drainage

If you are building your home on a hillside lot, the first necessity is a curtain drain that runs completely behind the house and carries any water that is flowing down the hill around the house and away below it. Even a fairly flat lot can also benefit from curtain draining. A curtain drain is usually fabricated by excavating a trench down to a depth below the lowest level of the house footing, filling the trench with a good draining material like crushed rock. The curtain drain line must be constructed uphill from the house foundation. In some cases, it is constructed in the same excavation that you do for your footing and foundation wall. In this case, the foundation becomes the downhill side of the curtain drain.

Curtain drains also perform a function besides just diverting water. By diverting water, they stabilize the soil and keep it from retaining water. Soil that contains plenty of water becomes very unstable and can collapse in a landslide or mudslide. This is particularly true where the soil has high clay content. Once a hillside is stripped of its vegetation, it can be come like a big sponge holding large amounts of water. Improper curtain draining is the biggest reason that hillside structures or homes collapse.

To facilitate drainage, a perforated pipe is usually placed in the bottom of the trench. This helps the water drain away from the structure to the downhill side. The size of the trench and piping depends on the amount of water that is anticipated. Most curtain drains are about six inches wide and have four-inch drain piping. Make sure that your curtain drain is sized properly and that it is constructed properly. There should be no obstructions that can block, limit, or divert the flow of water where you do not want it to go. Obstructions might include any man made or natural object that can impede the flow of water through the drain line. Examples of such obstructions are large rocks, retaining walls, or even tree roots. If you have questions, a soil engineer can help you with the calculations necessary to design your curtain drain system properly. Other drainage on a building site may also be necessary to keep the land dry. These systems include, but are not limited to, roof drains, foundation drains, footing drains, floor drains, and water retention systems.

Roof drains collect the water that runs off an underground roof and divert it away from the structure. In underground houses, they are analogous to a gutter drain that collects the run-off water from a roof and diverts it away from the home. The initial roof cover of an underground home is usually a porous draining material, like crushed rock, which allows water running off the roof to drain quickly and be collected on the perimeter of the structure. From here, this water can be diverted to other drain systems such as the foundation or footing drain.

Foundation drains collect any water that comes up against the foundation and run it around the residence to the downhill side. Foundations drains are usually necessary with underground houses because the deep foundation acts like a river dam holding water behind the structure. A typical house foundation wall might be two or three feet but an underground home might have a ten-foot foundation wall. This is why curtain drains are sometimes combined with the foundations drains. Hillside lots almost always require foundation drains and curtain drains. Sometimes both drainage systems can be combined and sometimes they must be constructed separately. Footing drains run around the base of a home's footing and collect water at its lowest point to divert to the downhill side of the structure. Footing drains are often the last collection point for curtain, roof, and foundation drains collecting all the water from these drains and diverting it away from the structure.

Floor drains are not always necessary but may be important if your home sits in a low-lying area with poor drainage. In this case, the concrete floor is poured over a well draining material, like compacted sand, and water drains away from the floor slab through the fill material itself. Piping can also be run at the low point of the floor drainage fill to drain water more efficiently away from the floor.

When the water drained away from a structure becomes excessive, usually during times of heavy rainfall, you may need to install a storm water retention system on your property. A storm water retention system retains excessive storm water and releases it more slowly during times of low water flow. This is especially important in areas like Southern Texas that may have extremely heavy rainfall or land runoff during certain times of the year. Water retention systems act like a huge sponge storing the water that the system cannot divert fast enough during times of heavy water flow. This buffering system allows heavy rainwater to be collected and stored and release more slowly over time.

Storm retention systems usually consist of large pipes, made of concrete or steel, that are buried below the ground on the property. The size of these systems is another thing that is determined by the amount of water on the site during the heaviest water flows. Sometimes water retention is accomplished aboveground in large aboveground ponds called retention ponds. This is done very commonly in large residential developments, because water retention is cheaper aboveground than belowground.

If your lot sits in a basin with water draining in from all of the areas around it, you may have to come up with a special drainage plan, which might involve special drainage systems. Some of these systems involve collecting water in a sump, or temporary collection well, and pumping up to higher ground. In some cases, these drainage systems can be very complex. In rare cases, poor drainage can keep you from building on a lot altogether. Low lying marsh or wetlands do not provide a good building site for earth-sheltered homes. Most areas of the country also have laws that prohibit building in a declared wetland.

Remember water drainage is a big part of the expense of building an earth-sheltered home, so the easier your property is to drain, the less expensive drainage will be. Because of the importance of drainage, it is also a poor place to cut costs. Money spent on an excellent water drainage system is good insurance — it will also provide good piece of mind.

Waterproofing Membranes

After the drainage system, the next most important part of water handling is creating a water-impermeable membrane on the floor, foundation, and roof structure of your underground building. Waterproofing each part of an underground home is important because even with proper drainage, water will still be present and this moisture can even creep through porous concrete over time. The safest thing to do is to make sure that water cannot, under any circumstances, penetrate these barriers.

On the floor system this is usually accomplished by pouring the concrete floor slab over a 6 mil poly-sheeting in areas where the floor slab is not insulated. In areas where floor insulation is required, the insulation itself is a water barrier.

On foundation walls and roof surfaces the standard practice for water protection below grade in conventional homes is to paint the concrete surfaces with a petroleum tar roof coating. This tar coating is often supplemented with layers of polyethylene sheeting. For an underground home, however, this practice is entirely insufficient. The hydrostatic forces, or water pressures, on earth-sheltered homes are much greater than those found in conventional housing because these homes usually lie deeper in the ground, so a much better system of waterproofing must be found. This is where modern building technology can really help. Modern polymeric compounds can be used to provide the same type of water impermeable barriers used for pools, underground water storage, and decorative ponds.

All good water-proofing products involve sheets of material that are used to coat the substrate. This is opposed to paint on products, which only coat the substrate to be protected. Stay clear of the paint-on-only products, because they are considered a damp proofing product not a waterproofing one. They are not as durable and cannot provide sufficient water protection.

One of my favorite waterproofing products is W.R. Grace's Bituthene® water membrane. This product is a petroleum-based, multi-layer polymer compound that can be used to coat vertical or horizontal surfaces and it provides a very durable water-proof membrane. It is relatively easy to install and inexpensive. It consists of two cross-laminated layers of polyethylene over a 60 mil layer of stick rubber bitumen material. This product is used very commonly in the roofing industry to seal up areas where roof penetrations are made. The sticky surface is protected by a coating of plastic that peels off for application. Other companies manufacture similar products, and there are also many other good water-proofing products available. Roof penetrations are commonly made for skylights, plumbing vents, and stove chimneys.

Polypropylene (PP), polyurethane (PU), polyethylene (PE), polyvinyl chloride (PVC), and polybutalene (PB) all have proven successful as an underground waterproofing material. Butyl rubber sheets, neoprene, and EPDM rubber sheeting can also be used as waterproof sheeting. Also many modified roofing product sheetings can be applied on the roof of your residence to properly waterproof them. The key is finding something that is completely waterproof, very durable, and fairly simple and cost effective to apply.

For superior waterproofing, both PVC and nylon reinforced polypropylene are extremely effective. PVC in 30 or 40 mil thicknesses is used as decorative pond liners and tile shower liners. Nylon reinforced polypropylene is used as float liners and for tenting materials. Both products retail for about $1 per square foot of area covered and when combined with an asphalt emulsion glue should do a very good job of keeping water out. Both can be heat- or solvent-sealed at the joints.

Modern torch down roofing products are also an excellent waterproofing product for the roof structure. Many consist of a very durable asphalt fiber reinforced material that is inexpensive to purchase and can be easily applied. They are installed with a flame torch and heat sealed seams and when properly installed can even hold standing water.

Some of these products rely on advanced polymer chemistry to create long chains of chemical bonds that serve this function admirably. Some water-proofing systems involve placing long monolithic sheets with special heat-treated or chemically glued seams. These can be very complicated and are best applied only by professionals. Whatever system you decide to use, research your options carefully.

Saving Money on Waterproofing

Saving money on waterproofing is possible, but remember this is a very important part of your structure, so do not skimp here if you do not have to. Good water-proofing coatings can last a long time, and save you plenty of money on maintenance later on.

One way of saving money is to do the installation of the waterproofing yourself. Most of the poly products mentioned above are fairly easy to install yourself. Most come with an installation manual that, if followed carefully, will lead to great results.

Choosing a product that is easier to self-install may save you money in the long run. Some of these products involve hot applications with a torch and some involve chemical primers to prepare the surface and keep things bonded properly. Some just involve working with very sticky materials. Whatever systems you use, be sure to follow the installation instructions carefully and ask for help when you need it. You do not have to be an expert to install water-proofing products, you just have to work carefully.

If you do hire someone else to do your waterproofing, some ways to save money include:

- Hire a specialty waterproofing contractor rather than a general contractor.
- Get three estimates and compare the bids.
- Get good references from anyone you select.
- Examine the contract carefully.
- Beware of deals that seem too good to be true.

Following these steps will assure that you get the best job for the best price. One reported problem with any type of waterproof coating seems to be ants eating their way through the coating. In some parts of the country, there have been reports of fire ants eating their way through $\frac{1}{8}$-inch sheets of synthetic rubber. The best preventative step here to protect your waterproofing membrane is to keep the ants away from it.

Insulation

Insulating your home is the best way to protect it from temperature extremes and condensation. Installation reduces the amount of heat loss on a structure. By reducing temperature extremes, installation can also keep condensation from occurring inside your residence. Condensation occurs when warm, moist air comes in contact with a cold surface. Insulation keeps these cold surfaces from forming, thereby reducing condensation effects. Insulation on a typical underground home will be found in the floors, walls, and roofing.

There were three types of insulation commonly found in conventional structures; hard board insulation, soft bat insulation, and soft fill insulation. All three types of insulation serve the same function. That is to reduce the flow of heat from one area to another. In conventional homes, soft insulation is usually found in the wall cavities, in the ceiling space, and sometimes in the subfloor cavities. This insulation serves to prevent the flow of heat from the warm interior of the home to the cold exterior.

Earth-sheltered homes generally lack structural cavities, which mostly precludes the use of soft fill insulation materials. Most underground homes will rely much more heavily on hard board installation materials or the insulation capacity of the construction material used. Hard board insulation can be applied to the roof surfaces, wall surfaces, and under the floor slab to provide thermal protection. Construction materials like earth bags, used tires, and other alternate materials can also provide insulation capacity to an underground structure. The insulation of an earth-filled tire, for example, may not be as good as polystyrene, but it is much cheaper. When these alternate materials are used some of the primary insulation may be eliminated or reduced.

In underground homes, insulation generally serves to limit heat loss from the warm interior space to the cooler ground temperatures. It also sometimes serves to limit cooling effects of the earth in the summer months. Because of the differences in the temperature gradients between an earth-sheltered home and conventional home, the function of insulation also becomes much more important in reducing condensation effects. The temperature of the earth is a fairly constant 50 to 60 degrees all year round. In the summer months, this means that without insulation your foundation wall can also be around 55 degrees. The rapid cooling of moist, warm air by a cool foundation wall can cause moisture to condense and appear on these types of surfaces. This is the same thing that happens when you see beads of water appearing on the outside of a cold glass of lemonade on a warm, humid summer day. Insulation reduces these effects by creating less sharp temperature gradients. When there is less of a difference in temperature from the surface of an object to the air, the process of condensation is reduced.

The two most common hard board insulation materials are polystyrene and polyurethane insulation boards. Polystyrene insulation board is manufactured from the same type of material used to manufacture Styrofoam cups. Long chains of the styrene molecule are linked together to create polystyrene. Polystyrene board consists of tiny beads of polystyrene that are expanded using hot steam and pressure into solid piece of insulation board. Polystyrene has an excellent R-value and is very resistant to heat transfer. Polystyrene insulation board can be manufactured to almost any shape, but usually comes in 4-foot by 6-foot sheets of various thicknesses. It is very resistant to water damage. Polystyrene can be submerged in water for very long periods of time with low rates of water absorption or damage to the material. The concrete floats that I used to manufacture, mentioned in an earlier chapter, had a core of polystyrene. In Europe and Japan, they use large polystyrene blocks to actually insulate and support roadbeds that cross marshy, permafrost ground.

Polyurethane insulation board is manufactured from long chains of the urethane molecule. It also sometimes goes by the name of polyisocyanate. Manufactured polyurethane insulation board is filled with tiny bubbles that help it become a good insulation material. Polyurethane insulation board also comes in 4-foot by 8-foot sheets of various thicknesses. The insulation value depends on the thickness of the board. The sheets can easily be applied to wall or roof surfaces to provide insulation. Polyurethane insulation board has less resistance to water absorption and damage. It is therefore not generally used in areas of continuous water submersion.

Polyurethane can also be sprayed on as a solid foaming product. It can also be applied as a liquid without any foam bubbles. This liquid will later harden into solid polyurethane. In its solid form, polyurethane is sometimes found used as a coating for the bed of pickup trucks. Rhino® brand truck bed liners are made of polyurethane. Solid polyurethane can also be used as a protective rubber industrial floor liner.

Foaming polyurethane insulation can be sprayed on surfaces or in cavities to provide insulation. It can also be used to seal around plumbing and electrical fixtures that penetrate an opening. Sold in spray cans, foaming polyurethane insulation can be applied to almost any surface.

Floor insulation

In some parts of the country, floor insulation is probably not necessary. Warmer areas may require only 6 mils of polyethylene sheeting under them to protect the floor slab. In colder areas, at least an inch of extruded polystyrene foam board should be placed under the floor slab. If you are planning on installing an in-floor heating, even more floor insulation may be required. This will protect your floor heating system from losing heat to the cooler ground. Local building codes should tell you exactly what the floor insulation requirements are in your area.

Wall insulation

The insulation installed below grade on an earth-sheltered home is universally installed on the external surface of the wall outside the water-proofing layer. This is because it is protected on the exterior surface from mechanical damage and here it will provide the most effective protection from condensation. By reducing thermal gradients on the outside of the wall, there will be less of a difference on the interior surface to provide condensation.

Sidewall insulation below grade is usually at least 2 inches of extruded polystyrene board. This provides an insulation value of at least R-10 on the side walls. In areas of extreme permafrost and cold, 3 inches of polystyrene may be advisable. Again, the thickness of this insulation is usually determined by local building codes. Insulation boar can be glued or taped over the exterior wall prior to backfill. No penetrating fasteners should ever be used to attach this material below grade. Both polystyrene and polyurethane panels can be easily cut and placed.

On the side walls, insulation board provides insulation and condensation protection. It also provides protection of the waterproof membrane from freeze-thaw cycles, which could potentially damage it. Polyurethane board, which has a slightly higher R-value per inch, can also be used as an insulation board when it is not exposed to water submersion. As mentioned previously, polyurethane board is less resistant to water damage and should never be used in conditions of water submersion.

Roof insulation

Because an earth cover does not provide a high-insulation value, roof insulation is almost always a requirement in underground structures. The amount of roof insulation will be determined by your local building codes. Most building codes require about an insulation value of R-30 to R-40 for roof structure. As previously discussed, dry earth has an R-value of around one per inch, but rather than covering your residence with 30 to 40 inches of earth, it is much better to supplement the earth cover with hard board insulation. The combination of insulation credit that you get for your superstructure with its earth cover and insulation board will usually require you to install from four to eight inches of polystyrene or polyurethane insulation board. Again, this insulation will be installed over the water-proofing membrane. Because roof areas are usually well drained, polyurethane board is used more commonly as a roof insulation. It is generally more expensive but has an R-value about 50 percent greater than polystyrene board insulation. Rigid foam insulation sometimes comes with a tongue and groove interlock that allows the insulation board to be installed as a continuous surface. Again when installing this board, it is important to glue or ballast the board to your roof surface and not use any penetrating fasteners that could damage your water-proofing system. Any penetrations through the roof surface must also be sealed around the insulation board. Bituthene® is also a very good material for this purpose. Ideally, your roofing insulation should be covered as soon as it is practical to do so. If not, these sheets of material might blow away or become damaged. Ballasting or covering the panels with a heavy material like gravel or stone can be used to keep the panels in place until your roof backfill is accomplished.

Saving Money on Insulation

There are several ways to save money on insulation. The first is by sourcing the material carefully. Sources for insulation differ greatly in their pricing schedules. When ordering a house load of insulation, costs should be significantly lower than picking up a small load. Several dealers that specialize specifically in providing insulation and drywall materials can be found in most areas. Hard board insulation can sometimes be bought directly from the manufacturer at a huge discount. Remember most of these types of materials can be damaged if not carefully protected. Damaged insulation will have dents or holes poked in it or may have absorbed excessive moisture. Inspect your insulation when it is delivered for damage, because damaged insulation will not work properly.

The best way to get a good price on your insulation package is to have a complete material list that specifies every piece of insulation you will need. Take this list to several product sources and ask for their best bid on your project. Smart negotiations with good product sources can usually save you significant amounts of money. Remember to always use competition to drive the price of your insulation package as low as possible.

Another way to save money on insulation involves being creative with your code compliance. Most building codes specify a standard R-value workflow. Some builders just build to the standard specification. Most code ordinances, however, have provisions for reducing the standard installation values based on your building shell. What this means is that by doing some simple calculations you may be able to reduce the amount or type of insulation in your walls or ceilings based on how you build the whole structure. For example, if your residence has a reduced number of windows, something that is very common in earth-sheltered homes, you may be able to take credit for the reduced heat loss with reduced window areas. Several building constraints allow you to apply extra energy credits to the value of your structure and reduce the overall insulation required. The cost savings of using a building-based shell rather than installing the standard installation packages can be significant. If your building codes specify an R-value of 40 in the roof, but you are able to reduce this to an R-value of 33 because of reduced window area, savings can be significant. In this particular example, the difference between R-40 insulation and R-33 installation on a 2,000-square-foot house is about $488. If your building codes allow you the option of taking building shell credits, always look at them to see if it is possible to reduce the amount of insulation you might need.

Ventilation

The ventilation in conventional homes is usually quite good. In fact, in some cases it is actually too great. Air leaks around doors and windows and through small cracks in walls allow air from the outside of the house to flow inside. These normal leaks are significant enough to provide excellent ventilation for most homes. With underground homes the situation is entirely different. Because walls and roofing are covered very tightly with earth, ventilation in earth- sheltered homes can be a problem. The flow of air through an underground home is severely reduced. Though this keeps dust out, it also allows air to stagnate and is not healthy.

Managing the quality of your air in your underground home needs to be carefully thought out so that the number of air exchanges will make the home comfortable and reduce its humidity or moisture content. Fortunately there are many good ways to assure good ventilation in an earth-sheltered home.

The first way to assure good ventilation in an underground home is merely to provide some form of mechanical vent that allows air to travel between the outside and the inside of your residence. In its simplest form this can be a passive vent that is manually opened and closed just like a window. This allows fresh air into the residence. A more complicated version of venting might include some form of mechanical air movement such as a ventilation fan. Here air movement could be increased dramatically to provide ventilation. Automatic ventilation can also be incorporated into your heating and cooling system. Heat exchangers and simpler mechanical heaters can be set up to allow mechanical forced air ventilation according to a prescribed schedule. Such ventilation is fairly inexpensive to operate. A 2,500-square-foot house with a ventilation fan running constantly will only add about two or three dollars to your monthly power bill.

The problem with letting outside air into your home, however, is that this air is usually much colder. Letting this air into your house can cause a loss of heat during the ventilation process. It is like trying to ventilate your house by just opening the front door. Ventilation without heat loss can be accomplished using a simple mechanical air-to-air heat exchanger. An air exchanger works by allowing warm air from the interior of a residence to travel to the outside and cold exterior air to travel into a residence. During this process the warmth from the interior air leaving the house is transferred very efficiently to the cold air being brought in. In this way while the air is exchanged, heat is conserved. Simple mechanical air-to-air heat exchangers have actually been used in conventional homes for many years. They work on a simple physical principle similar to the radiator in your car. The radiator of your car is essentially an air to water heat exchanger. In this case, hot engine heat is exchanged via the medium of the coolant in your radiator with the colder air.

If you live in a colder climate an air-to-air heat exchangers should be an important part of your ventilation system. Air exchange systems can be mechanically set up for between eight hundred and two thousand dollars. Because it is important to not only ventilate, but balance this ventilation these types of systems are usually installed by heating contractors.

Managing Humidity

Managing the ventilation of your underground home is not the only important consideration. The air quality is greatly enhanced by maintaining the proper humidity. Humidity is the amount of water that air holds. Warm air has the ability to hold more moisture than cold air. When warm moist air is cooled, water is released in the form of condensation. The ideal humidity of a home is about 45 percent relative humidity. Humidity below 30 percent is considered too dry. Such levels can lead to dry throats and noses, which can cause colds and other health-related problems. Too little humidity like this can actually do physical damage to your home. The drying effects of the air can cause joints to shrink and cracks in drywall plaster and even pianos to go out of tune. Telltale signs of low humidity include high static electricity, itchy skin, a dry throat or sinuses, and other respiratory problems.

High humidity or humidity in excess of 50 percent can also be a source of problems in your home. High levels of moisture in the air can leak and can be a breeding ground for mold, rot, and pest such as termites and cockroaches. Excess humidity can also be a source of condensation, which can cause paint to flake, and make wallpaper peel. The combination of high humidity and heat in warmer climates provides an optimal environment for mold growth. Mold spores, which are everywhere in the air, can settle out on a moist surface and reproduce. Symptoms of moist air include a sultry feel or heaviness to the air, condensation, or mold growth.

Dealing with less-than-ideal humidity levels

Dry air is usually more common in cold, Northern climates and warm moist air is common in the humid South. Surprisingly most homes contain a great many indoor moisture sources. Cooking, drying clothes, taking a shower, and even breathing add moisture to the air. Because of this, humidity control is very important in any home but becomes much more important in underground homes with their tighter air seals and controlled airflows. The secret to humidity control is keeping the moisture level of the air at its optimal setting.

If your home has dry air, water can be added to the air with a humidifier, which adds water vapor to your air. Humidifiers can be simple standalone units costing $50 to $200 or whole-house humidifier units that automatically sync with the whole-house heating system. Dry air is very common in homes that are heated by wood burning stoves. A simple, common remedy to the drying effects of a wood stove consists of placing a kettle or pot of water on the stove when it is being used. The slowly evaporating water vapor will fill the air as the stove heats and increase humidity.

More common than dry air in some areas is air that has high humidity. High humidity can be controlled using a dehumidifier. Dehumidifiers can be $200 to $400 standalone units or whole-house systems, which can cost upward of $1,000. Standalone units about the size of a large microwave oven can keep a large room dehumidified. Whole-house units can be tied into your existing heating system and work automatically as the home is heated.

Most people never seriously consider the effects of humidity on their health and comfort but if you are able to identify whether your home has low or high humidity, correcting the problem can benefit your health and add much more comfortable feel to your home.

Saving Money on Ventilation

In some areas of home construction it is more difficult to save money than others. Ventilation is probably one of those areas. Keeping your home well ventilated and controlling its humidity probably will result in long-term health savings. Buying efficient models of air-control equipment can also save you energy in the long run. Energy Star appliances, such as Energy Star rated de-humidifiers, can cost more initially but over their lives can save hundreds of dollars on your energy bill. In any case finding the right appliance at the best price is the best strategy to save money on ventilation.

Summary

Very unglamorous, but very important — this can be said about the elements of waterproofing, insulating and ventilation an underground home. When done properly, all of these elements can add comfort to your home. The peace of mind of having no water infiltration problems can never be underestimated. The comfort of a well-insulated home can likewise never be undersold, and the joys of having adequate and efficient ventilation can never be over emphasized. The proper handling of condensation and humility, though critical in conventional homes, is essential in earth-sheltered homes. Nowhere else has modern technology had such a great influence on the home building process than in these three areas.

Before the era of modern waterproofing products, all structures had water problems, today none have to. High R-value insulation can eliminate condensation and provide comfort all year. Efficient air handling equipment can bring humidity levels into the perfect range and provide clean quality air at an affordable cost.

Chapter 9

The Icing on the Cake:
Finishes and Amenities

"Art is never finished, only abandoned."
— Leonardo Da Vinci

For most people one of the most exciting parts of home construction is finishing the inside of their home. Some realize this is always a process and a home is always a work in progress. Seeing all the pieces finally come together and create a finished product is a very satisfying feeling. Unfortunately, finishing a home also involves many complicated decisions. What color should you paint each room? What type of kitchen counters should you use? What rooms should be carpeted and what rooms should have wood floors? What type of wood should the cabinets be made out of? All these and many other questions must be answered before you can move in and enjoy your underground home. Making these decisions can be challenging but it can also be very satisfying as all the parts of your house finally come together and it becomes a home.

Doors and Windows

Doors and windows become the accent of any good home. The types of doors you use may depend on many things. Exterior doors are usually much heavier and have a solid core. Exterior doors can be made of wood, steel, or other composite materials such as fiberglass or plastic. Exterior doors can also be decorative. An ornate decorative front door can add class to a residence but it can also add hundreds of dollars to its price. Interior doors are usually hollow core, which makes them lighter and easier to open, and close. Interior doors can be veneered or constructed of real wood. The type and style of door that you choose usually reflects your personal tastes and preferences. It can also reflect your pocketbook. The door and hardware packages for most homes typically runs from $2,500 to $4,000. Underground homes usually have fewer exterior doors. Because exterior doors are much more expensive than interior doors, it can reduce your door budget significantly.

Modern windows can add a great deal of class and style to a new home. Windows can be constructed of metal, wood, or plastic. Different styles allow a great deal flexibility in the design and construction of your home. Because of the reduced exterior wall area, underground homes usually have fewer windows than conventional homes due. This means that your choice of windows becomes even more important. Windows act as both a functional element to allow light and air into a home and as a design element to provide a certain look and style to the exposed areas of your home. Many different sources for windows exist and different window styles and constructions are shipped from every area of the country.

Windows can also be another source of energy savings. Because they are constructed of glass, which is a very poor insulator, home windows are the single largest source of heat loss to any home. This is why modern windows are constructed with double or triple panes; each window has more than one sheet of glass that makes it up. The space between the panes is filled with an inert gas such as nitrogen or argon to eliminate heat transfer and make the window more energy efficient. Original single pane glass windows had an R-value of about 0.91. Modern double and triple paned energy-efficient windows can have R-values of up to three. This may not sound like much but it represents a significant savings in energy loss. Information from **www.finehomebuilding. com** shows that the average house in Madison, Wisconsin could save approximately $200 per year by replacing single pane glass windows with double pane low E. argon-filled windows.

Doors and windows are a significant place to save money on a new home. The difference between standard and custom windows and doors is extremely significant. A standard factory manufactured door may run $300 to $400 but a door can run $2,000 to $3000. The standard plastic window package for a home can run about $2,000, but windows can run closer to $10,000. The style, type, and material of your window or door can have a very large influence on its price. Door and window suppliers also differ greatly in what they charge for their product. Secondhand or used doors and windows can also be obtained quite cheaply. Some of these can have even more class than custom fabricated items. Choose carefully and avoid spending money on custom items that are not absolutely necessary. Remember, you can always add a more ornate or decorative front door at a later date.

Interior Wall Finishes

The standard interior wall finish for a conventional home is sheet rock or drywall. The reason for this is that this gypsum-filled paper product is extremely resistant to fire. In candle lit old colonial homes around the turn of the last century, fires were extremely common. Log and wood homes, once they caught fire, would burn to the ground extremely rapidly. Mid century homes constructed of plaster and wood lath added a layer of plaster protecting the wooden structure. This kept fires from consuming a home so quickly. Modern conventional homes incorporate 4-foot by 8-foot sheets of gypsum drywall over all the wood framing of a home. This adds a layer of fire protection to every modern home. This "sheet rock" slows any home fires down to the point where they can be controlled by the local fire department.

Another advantage of sheet rock is that it is extremely cheap material that can be installed fairly quickly and efficiently. Nailed or screwed over wood framing studs, the joints are still sealed with a modern plaster spackling compound. The flat surface of drywall can also be textured to resemble the peel of an orange, heavy stucco, or many different kinds of stippled or knocked-down surfaces. In conventional homes, drywall is probably still the best option. Underground homes offer other creative options.

Because earth-shelter walls are usually constructed of concrete or earth-filled bags they are extremely fire resistant already. These surfaces can be left unfinished or textured the same way drywall is textured. This is a very practical option as it saves the time and expense of drywalling the home. Of course concrete or earth-bag walls can also be "furred" or framed out with thin non-structural framing like 2-inch by 2-inch lumber and then sheet rocked or covered with drywall. Once you have a finished surface, wall treatments can include texturing, painting, and wallpapering.

The biggest way to save money on wall treatments is to do them yourself. Texturing, painting, and wallpapering are easy ways to finish an interior wall and can be easily learned by anyone. A word of warning, though: Drywall is not something to be attempted by the amateur. It is a very difficult process to learn and can turn out looking extremely horrible if you do not know what you are doing.

Ceiling Finishes

The ceiling of conventional houses are almost always done with drywall. This can be textured much like a wall surface or coated with a texturing aerial. Before the 1970s, this texturing material in some cases was actually particles of asbestos. This asbestos texture presented no problem because it was usually sealed with paint. Many older houses, however, had to have special contractors remediate asbestos ceilings by sealing the house off and coming in and removing it with special processes. With their sheltered homes most, unfinished ceilings consist of concrete. This concrete can be left unfinished, textured, or covered with a false or suspended ceiling. You may even want to leave the original ceiling unfinished until a later time.

Skylights and Light Tubes

One of the most exciting finishes to an underground home includes skylights and light tubes. These have been previously discussed as a way to bring outside light into the home. Skylights or roof windows can be added over any room to bring direct sunlight into that room. Skylights can be tinted or non-tinted, have an opening or be sealed, and can even include blinds for shutting out the light during certain times of the day. Light tubes, as previously discussed, are also an excellent way to bring outside light into the home. They differ from skylights in that the light can be bent and made to travel fairly long distances into the house. They are usually installed in one area of the roof and can bring light to a room that is 15 feet away. Light tubes also differ in the fact that they only bring light — and not a view — into the room. With a skylight you can actually look outside and see the sky. With a light tube, you only see exterior light. Both these amenities are highly recommended in an underground home. Both can be installed at a later date, but it is less expensive to install them when you are building the home.

Finished Flooring

Many different kinds of flooring finishes are also an option with an underground home. If you have a concrete floor, it can be left unfinished or it can be covered with different types of materials. One material that is very popular is clay or ceramic tile. Tile can actually be glued to a concrete floor and the joints can be filled with a mortar material to provide a beautifully aesthetic look. Tile is durable, fireproof, and offers an extremely wide range of design options for almost any taste. Natural rock slate can also be used as a floor covering. Natural stone slates come in a wide range of colors and textures. The advantages of using slate or tile as a floor covering is that it does not diminish the value of your floor's thermal mass. This is particularly important if you are relying on solar heating. Another material that can be used for flooring finishes is wood flooring. This includes the traditional hardwood flooring options like oak, cherry wood, or maple as well as some of the more modern wood flooring materials. A recent addition to the wood flooring options is bamboo flooring, which can be laid over a concrete floor and provides a very durable and attractive finish. Bamboo flooring is a fairly new option and still more expensive than the traditional hardwood floor.

A wide range of imitation wood floor coverings also are manufactured today that can be installed over a concrete floor. These include simulated wood parquet flooring products that have many brand names. These offer the advantage of being less expensive, easy to install, and very durable. Most are installed over the floor as a floating system that allows thermal expansion and contraction.

Traditional floor coverings also include carpeting and vinyl sheet covering. Carpeting comes in a wide range of prices and appearances. Short nap commercial carpeting is fairly inexpensive and extremely durable. It is also easy to clean. Longer nap residential carpeting can provide many different textures, and comes in a wide range of prices and colors. It is fairly durable and harder to keep clean. Throw rugs or Persian carpeting can also be used as area floor coverings. Sheet vinyl or vinyl tiles can also be installed over a concrete floor fairly inexpensively. Most of these products are fairly durable and very easy to clean.

Conventional floor coverings usually include carpets in most living rooms and bedrooms and vinyl floor coverings in bathrooms and kitchens. The reason for this is that the vinyl is more resistant to water than carpeting.

Saving money on flooring finishes usually involves finding the best source for the material. There is a huge difference in price between different suppliers of carpet and vinyl products. Discount flooring companies sometimes offer deals that seem too good to be true on remnant carpeting or carpeting pieces that have been left over from a large project. Factory seconds on floor coverings can also be obtained from some dealers. When shopping for good deals be sure and know what you are getting and why it has been discounted. Normal carpeting prices also vary significantly depending on the style of the carpet. Typically, carpeting sells for between $18 and $28 a yard. As a builder, I often buy carpet from discounted commercial sources for $8 to $10 a yard. Most of these sources are available to someone who searches diligently for them. Discount sources for slate and tile also can be found in certain geographical areas of the United States. A friend of mine once saved thousands of dollars by driving to Mexico to pick up a trailer load of hand-crafted floor tile rather than buying it from the local retail outlet. Discount sources for hardwood flooring can also be found. Some hardwood floor installers offer discount sales during certain times of the year to keep their crews busy.

Another idea for saving money in your flooring costs is to buy the materials at the best price as a separate item and hire a specialty contractor to install the materials for you. Most large flooring companies hire out their work to a series of smaller flooring contractors who work independently and markup the price to you. By buying the material separately and placing an ad in the local paper for someone with the appropriate expertise, you might be able to save all of that markup on the specialty contractor's work. For example, carpeting can be purchased as a separate item and installed by a specialty contractor for $3 to $4 per yard. If you had this carpet installed by a typical flooring company, the work would include an additional markup on the price of the carpet, the specialty contractor's charges, and the total price for the work. When it is all added up this may include $5 to $8 more per yard for your carpet installation. The same is true with tile, slate, or wood floors. Specialty contractors usually can be found in most areas to help you with this work. Be sure to check references carefully and negotiate hard with your subcontractor, using competition to get the best price.

Millwork

The millwork in a home generally includes such things as door and floor trims, decorative woodwork, and cabinets. Trim work is usually done with hardwood or paper-laminated imitation hardwood. Millwork can be a very large part of your home finish budget. One of the bigger elements is the cost of kitchen and bathroom cabinets. Typical cabinet packages can range from $4,000 up to $30,000, depending on the style, type of wood, and hinge hardware. Custom cabinets, or cabinets made up as a custom product for your home, are generally much more expensive than stock order cabinets. With modern cabinet construction techniques, the difference in look has become less and less over the years. Stock cabinets purchased through large building outlets offer a wide range of styles and finishes to meet almost any taste. Most of these large building outlets even offer free layout, and materials are delivered directly to your site. Custom cabinet-supply shops also offer good packages. Many buy prefabricated doors from the same sources that the stock companies do and build custom boxes to fit your kitchen or bathroom layout. Installing the millwork is an area where you will want to be very careful, because appearances count. Improperly installed cabinets or floor trim can be a huge detriment to the look and feel of a finished home.

The best way to save money on cabinet packages is to negotiate the best deal with several different sources. Cabinet and millwork products usually have a higher markup and most sources are willing to negotiate to get your business. If you are not doing the work yourself, cabinet and millwork installation can also be best achieved by subcontracting to a specialty contractor. Because of the nature of the business, most areas of the country have many millwork subcontractors who would be willing to sell their services to an owner or builder. Using these subcontractors would be much less expensive than having a large building outlet markup the same company's work to you.

CASE STUDY: BEATING THE MISCONCEPTIONS

Jerry N. Hickok, President & CEO
Earth Sheltered Technologies, Inc
P.O. Box 5142
Mankato, MN 56001
www.earthshelteredtech.com
jnate@earthshelteredtech.com
est@earthshelteredtch.com
1-800-345-7203
507-345-8302 (FAX)

Jerry Hickok has spent more than 30 years in the design and marketing of earth-sheltered homes.

Over the years, he has found that the most important design consideration is the soil compaction and the positioning of the home on the property. A properly designed and situated home can use passive solar heating to do all of the home's heating. Hickok said they have homes in Minnesota that will never fall below 55 degrees, even mid-winter, without some form of cooling. This is because earth-sheltered homes require 25 percent of the energy of a conventional home, but much greater air exchanges because of the tightness of the home.

Hickok said the biggest problem with earth-sheltered homes is that most people have great misconceptions about how they work and are not willing to take the time to tour one. But his company, Earth Sheltered Technologies, works to get people to open up their minds, with 21 show homes across the nation open for touring.

Hickok, a huge proponent of earth-sheltered living, deals with many clients who think that underground homes will be dark, dank, and cold with mildew growing everywhere. "They have never seen one of our company's homes," he said. According to Hickok, earth-sheltered homes are far healthier to live in than conventional homes, primarily because of the types of materials these homes are constructed of. Wood-chipped and glued products out gas toxins that can be ingested by people living in the home.

Another common misconception is that underground homes are difficult to build and costly to finish. Jerry says earth-sheltered homes can be finished similarly to any conventional home. The cost will depend on what type of materials the owner selects. Just like conventional homes, you can buy kitchen cabinets for $1,800 or $18,000, Hickok said. Typical underground homes finish for approximately the same price as a medium-priced "stick-built" home. But, earth-sheltered homes will cost 80 percent less to live in.

One of the best testimonials of Earth Sheltered Technologies earth-sheltered homes is the level of customer satisfaction. Of the hundreds of homes Hickok's company has built, he said no one has been a bit unhappy with their home. Once clients have gotten past their misconceptions, they are sold on the product. For Hickok, there is not a better type of the home on the market today.

Other Considerations

A living roof

When planning for the finishing of your underground home, do not neglect the exterior surfaces. This includes any exposed exterior walls and the roof structure itself. One of the most exciting finishes offered with earth-sheltered housing is something called a living roof. Here, the earth used as a cover of 6 to 8 inches is planted and allowed to grow naturally.

To create a living roof, the original waterproof roof membrane is covered with hardboard insulation and this is covered with 2 to 3 inches of crushed gravel drainage material. The drainage material is then covered by drainage fabric, hay, or a straw mat and 5 to 6 inches of topsoil. The perimeter of your roof structure can be retained with moss or grass sod edges. The topsoil can then be planted with grass or wildflowers. The type of material that you plant on your roof will depend on what grows best in your area. Natural rain will keep the roof living and help the home blend into its natural surroundings much better. Living roofs can be left to grow naturally or mowed or pruned at your preference.

Thermal mass and solar heating

Another important consideration with solar heating involves the use of solar mass. Solar mass is effectively anything that is heated by the sun and releases its heat slowly. Many earth-sheltered homes use solar heating. Passive solar heating allows the sun to heat a home during the daylight hours, and the thermal mass allows a home to release the heat that it collects all day slowly during the unheated hours. You can think of it as a battery during the daylight hours, when the sun's heat charges the thermal mass battery with collected heat. During the non-heating collecting hours, this stored heat energy is released slowly into the house. With passive solar heating, many different things can serve as a solar mass. Concrete walls or floors can collect and slowly release heat. Black used-rubber tires stacked on a wall can also serve as a solar mass. Even dark colored barrels filled with water can be used to store the sun's energy. Everyone is familiar with how black asphalt can heat up during a hot summer day. Temperatures can actually be hot enough to fry an egg.

The proper use of the thermal mass is usually something that needs to be well thought out or engineered by someone with passive solar heating experience. A poorly designed system will store only a fraction of the sun's energy that is available or may store too much energy and actually keep a home too warm. A well-designed passive solar energy system includes balancing the energy input from the sun and the storage capacity and releasing rates of any collecting thermal mass. Properly balanced passive solar can be used as a primary heating source for your residence. Using the sun's heat can be an extremely efficient and economical method of heating.

Dealing with the Radon Monster

One of the disadvantages of living in an underground home that we have previously discussed is the hazard of radon gas. Radon is a naturally occurring radioactive gas that is odorless, colorless, and tasteless. It results from the deterioration of naturally occurring uranium in soil, rock, or water. Certain areas of the country can have higher concentrations of the gas but radon gas can be found in almost all areas of the country.

The primary danger of radon is that it is radioactive. When breathed in, the radioactive gas comes into contact with lung tissue and can lead to detrimental health effects such as lung cancer. It is estimated that approximately 20,000 lung cancer deaths in the United States occur each year as a result of exposure to radon gas. Radon exposure is not something that is unique to Earth-sheltered homes. Conventional homes can also have problems with radon.

The solution to taming the radon monster is conducting tests in your home for radon gas. The test kits are fairly inexpensive and can be obtained from companies on the Internet. The testing usually involves either a short term or long term test kit that is set up in your home to collect the radiation released by radon gas. Short-term tests can remain in your home from two to 90 days to monitor the air. They are then sent in for evaluation by a testing lab. Long-term testing occurs over a period of more than 90 days and probably gives a more accurate representation of radon gas levels. If you find the presence of radon gas in your home, radon reduction systems work very effectively and are not very expensive to implement. Some radon reduction systems can reduce radon levels in your home by up to 99 percent. With this efficiency, even very high levels of radon gas can be reduced to acceptable levels.

If you are building in a part of the country that has high radon content emitted by its soils, there are also radon-resistant construction techniques that can more effectively prevent radon from entering your home. When installed properly, these simple and inexpensive building techniques can be used to help reduce indoor radon to very low levels. Every new home should probably be tested for radon gas. If radon levels appear in excess of four picocuries per liter some form of remedial action should be taken.

Radon gas can penetrate your home many different ways. One way it typically penetrates a home is through the ground to air contact of the foundation wall. Radon gas can easily seep through cracks and holes in a foundation wall. Because radon gas is heavier than air, it is often trapped inside a home and becomes concentrated over time. Any home may have a radon problem regardless of how well sealed or ventilated it is. In fact, it is estimated that one out of every 15 homes in the United States has elevated radon gas levels. Radon gas can also penetrate a home through gaps around service pipes, construction joints, and cracks in your floor. Radon can also penetrate a home through well water. Radon gas absorbed by groundwater can be released when you take a shower or run the tap water, which can create a problem in schools, work offices, and public buildings, too.

Rather than fear radon, the important thing is to understand it. Understanding what parts of the country are more at risk, how to test for radon, and how to reduce it if it is found, are important in the building of any home.

Other Health Threats – Mold and Mildew

Another health threat, which is much more dangerous than radon gas, is the presence of mold or mildew in your home. Mold and mildew can be a problem in any type of home. Both mold and mildew belong to the same family of organism that mushrooms do. They are both a type of fungus, but there is no room for fungi in anyone's home. Fungi love to grow in areas that are warm and moist. Deprive them of warmth or moisture and you will keep them from growing and reproducing.

Most people's first encounter with mold or mildew occurs after a roof leak or water pipe leakage. Mold spore (or seed) is continuously present every place in the air. When it encounters a damp, warm place to grow, the reproductive spores produce long almost invisible microscopic threads called mycelium that burrow their way deeply into the infested surface. Homeowners become aware that a fungus is present when the mycelium threads produce a reproductive fruiting body that contains the fungi spores on infected surface. The fruiting body, not the actual fungus, is what is usually visible to the naked eye.

Mold and mildew fruiting bodies can be almost any color. Beautiful shades of bright yellow, red, and orange fungus fruits are sometimes found sprouting on drywall and carpeting. More common mildews and mold are seen growing in green, gray, and black spots on infected walls or ceilings. The color of the mold spore bodies depends on the type of mold or mildew that is present.

Recent concerns have been expressed that mold spores can present health hazards in your home. Certain types of mold and mildew spores have been found to contain chemical compounds that can irritate lungs or even cause severe allergies. Certain poisons in mold spores can even cause adverse health effects, ranging from depression to skin rashes and digestive problems. If you have mold in your home and notice any of the following conditions on the chart below you may have mold problems.

COMMON MOLD-RELATED HEALTH PROBLEMS

Sinus problems or infections

Dizziness

Allergic symptoms

Burning or itchy eyes, nose, or throat

Nausea

Digestive problems

Low-grade fever

Changes in your immune system

Fatigue or lack of energy

Depression

Memory loss or other neurological symptoms

An infamous black mold called Stachybotrys has had plenty of media attention lately as a cause of health problems and a source of lawsuits, and has caused a good deal of fear. Some people, out of fear, have come to think that any black mold is Stachybotrys, which is definitely not true. This particular type of fungus is extremely slow-growing. It takes a very long time to incubate and does not compete well with other types of fungus. The danger posed by it is in something called trichothecene mycotoxin satratoxin-H, which is produced by the fungus and poisonous if it is inhaled. The health effects can include flu-like symptoms, diarrhea, sore throats, and headaches. Although there are a variety of symptoms and illness that can result from mold, in very few instances are any of mold's toxic effects life-threatening.

Treating mold in your home

It is impossible for the average homeowner to tell what type of mold is growing in their home simply by looking at it. Because of this, all molds should be treated with equal disdain. If you have mold growing in your home, the sooner it leaves the better.

The presence of mold can be detected in a home by a musty smell. Approximately 95 percent of all homes with mold infestation have a musty smell. The other key symptom of mold infestation is the presence of a water leak, usually a roof or pipe leak, and condensation. Remember, molds love water. In fact they cannot live and reproduce without it. Unfortunately not all mold infestations are visible. Mold can live behind sheetrock, underneath moldings, or even beneath the planks of a wood floor. Any place there is moisture, there is the possibility you could find mold. Mold infestation has even commonly been found in air ducts, inside waste pipes, and on the underside of crawl space floors. The molds makes a living eating any organic content it can find, which includes wood, drywall, and sometimes even vinyl.

If you discover mold in your home the important thing is to eliminate it immediately. Fortunately most mold infestation can be alleviated fairly quickly by drying the area out and using a good mildewcide. Drying the area out may first include fixing any apparent source of water leakage or condensation. After eliminating the source of the moisture, the next step is to remove any latent water by ventilating the area with a large commercial fan for several days. Once dried, no mold can grow or reproduce. Applying a commercial mildewcide or disinfection solution will also help kill any mold that is present quickly. If you do not know where to find a commercial mildewcide, a solution of 3 parts water to 1 part bleach works equally well.

Moisture

In an all underground homes, the biggest hazard is always moisture. Making sure to keep water and condensation out of your home will assure that you never have a mold or mildew problem.

WHAT TO DO IF YOU HAVE A MAJOR WATER LEAK

A major water leakage like a broken water pipe can occur in almost any home at any time, but most people are very unprepared for such an occurrence. What do you do when the water supply hose on your washing machine breaks right after you leave on a one-week vacation? Most people come back from their vacation to a big surprise. In the week you were gone, the water has probably done extensive damage to your home and your walls are probably starting to be covered with mold.

The first thing to do is to sit down and take a deep breath — this type of occurrence happens very often. It happens so often that most home insurance companies cover water damage claims as a routine part of their business. Many water damage contractors specialize in cleaning up and repairing water damage. Most water damage contractors are also mold remediation contractors and are experienced in locating and assessing home damage. They can take the mess of a large water damage cleanup to make the process much simpler for you.

Water damage repair specialists use the same mold remediation techniques that homeowners can use. They are just better at it. Larger ventilation fans, commercial mildewcide, and expertise in finding and eliminating water wherever it can be, make them probably a better option if you have a large water leak. Large water damage also sometimes involves major repairs. This can include replacement of damaged drywall or rotten wood. This type of damage repair is probably best left to the experts. So the next time you come home from vacation to find a big water surprise, the first thing you should do is call your insurance company.

Home Pests

Since the day man started living in caves, it seems we have had to compete against natural creatures for a home. Nowadays, instead of competing against saber tooth tigers, we find competition of a much less dangerous sort. Wild pests can be a problem with any home but earth-sheltered homes seem to be a bit more vulnerable because they usually lie much closer to the natural environment. Groundhogs, gophers, and moles have sometimes mistaken covered roofs for natural ground. Ground nesting birds have been known to find the perimeter of the earth-shelter roof as an irresistible place to build a nest. As we have seen in a previous section, burrowing ants can sometimes can cause damage to an underground home's waterproofing system by eating into it. Vegetable-garden-robbing deer have even been known to raid rooftop gardens sometimes when an underground homeowner least expects it.

Most pest problems can be solved quite simply by recognizing the natural creatures that share our area of the neighborhood and dealing with them kindly and appropriately. One earth-shelter owner tells the story of a honeybee infestation on the eaves of her underground house. Rather than calling a commercial pest inspector she called a beekeeping friend who vacuumed all the bees up in a vacuum cleaner and left thanking her for the new sources of honey.

Summary

Just like eating a dessert after a meal, finishing a home is the best part of the construction process. Although many different decisions need to be made during this time, it is one of the most exciting parts of building a home. These decisions are important ones because they will determine your lifestyle in your new home for years to come. But, remember that there is no right or wrong way to finish a home. Each owner or builder will make his or her own choices depending on the preferences he or she has developed. Some are more comfortable with textured sheetrock wall, but others are more comfortable with unfinished concrete. Whatever your preferences, remember that nothing is every permanent and all things can be changed over time. An unfinished room can always be finished later, and a room finished one way can always be remodeled to something different later on. Finish your home the way you want it to be now, and let the future take care of itself.

Chapter 10

Home Sweet Home:
What to Expect Living in an
Earth-Sheltered Home

> *"Only as high as I reach can I grow, only as far as I seek can I go, only as deep as I look can I see, only as much as I dream can I be."*
> — *Karen Ravn, author*

After talking with many underground homeowners, the general impression I get is that living in an earth-sheltered home is not much different than living in a regular house. The biggest differences seem to involve the benefits inherent in using the earth as a natural protection and the energy saving aspects. As discussed earlier, the primary and most important difference is in a homeowner's energy bills. Although living quietly and comfortably below the earth may not appeal to everyone, to some it has a very strong appeal. When combined with modern building technologies and a green emphasis, earth sheltered-housing offers a way to give back to the earth some of what each one of us is taking from it every day. Recent concerns about energy and environmental damage and the impact we are having on finite resources have driven many to start considering this type of building more seriously. The creativity of many who have taken on the challenge of building an earth-shelter has paved the way for many more to follow. As energy costs continue to increase, it is likely that we will see even more types of alternative housing constructed.

Although the number of earth-sheltered homes in the United States still numbers less than hundreds of thousand (compared to hundreds of millions of conventional homes), these numbers will continue to grow. Most of these homes are built by creative owners or builders who have decided the benefits outweigh the risks. One thing that cannot be ignored in the trend of building earth-shelters is the idea that people can look at homes much differently than they used to be looked at, instead of a home being just four walls and a roof with comfortable amenities inside.

The Autonomous House

Strictly speaking conventional housing today is a great waste of resources. Many homes are built without giving much thought to the conservation of resources and energy. Building houses based on the principle of sustainable resources and green architecture is not a new idea. More primitive societies had to use their resources with much more utility because they recognized they were limited. It is only recently that modern societies have realized resources are still limited and need to be used wisely if we are to protect our future.

More of an interest is being given to something referred to quite eloquently as the "autonomous house." This is a house that pollutes the environment less and does not squander its valuable resources. It is a well thought out approach to homebuilding that should see an increased following in the years and decades to come.

First outlined in a book "The Autonomous House" by Brenda and Robert Vale in 1975, the idea had very broad public appeal. It offers suggestions for building homes that do not pollute the Earth. The main tenant is that current housing cannot continue in the wasteful fashion it has allowed to in the past. That it is possible to live in a less expensive manner with lower utilities bills and a much more eco-friendly style of living. This is a message that has a very strong appeal for many today.

The principles of the autonomous house are very closely aligned with the principle of most underground builders today. By using good function, technology, and design the standard house can be converted into an eco-house.

CASE STUDY: DRY LIVING UNDERGROUND

Ray Wetherholt
Wetherholt and Associates, Inc.
P.O. Box 816
Kirkland, WA 98083
www.wetherholt.com
rayw@wetherholt.com
(425) 822-8397

In the Pacific Northwest, earth-sheltered homes are less common than other parts of the country. The weather is much moister in the Northwest, and waterproofing these types of homes is more difficult here. About 29 years ago, Ray Wetherholt, a licensed PE working at a construction materials testing lab, began his dream home south of Monroe, a suburb of Seattle. Working from out-of-pocket funds and doing much of the construction himself over a two-and-a-half-year period, he created a 900 square-foot, one bedroom, concrete, underground home.

Later, when Wetherholt became a waterproofing and roofing consultant, he was not scared by the Northwest water. Using a practical asphalt coating on the walls, he torched down roofing on the topping slab over the precast roof panels and used mold-resistant paint to make his water problems minimal. A well-engineered drainage system, along with with the proper insulation to prevent interior condensation, provided the finishing touches. Though his techniques worked at the time, Wetherholt said that if he knew then what he knows now, he might have constructed his home a little differently. The finished result had only one leak problem, which was in a skylight area and that was easily fixed.

Waterproofing aside, Wetherholt's general impression of living in his underground home was that it was just about the same as living in a conventional home. One of the things that helped ease his transition to earth-sheltered living was situating the house on the property in such a way as to provide a very nice view of the surrounding scenery. Another thing that helped was a home design that included 8-foot ceilings in the back bedroom and a 10-foot entry and living room ceiling. Wetherholt also included several skylights to let natural light in, and a light well in the bedroom also doubled as an emergency fire exit.

Wetherholt used a wood stove to heat his home and he noticed right away that the home would warm quickly and cool slowly, which made it fairly comfortable and inexpensive to heat. Because his front wall was constructed of sliding glass doors over a low frame wall, a lot of light was let into the house. His roof was grass that he mowed himself, even though it was placed over the waterproofing and insulation. Home maintenance, overall, was pretty minimal, and the costs of living underground were really reasonable, Wetherholt said.

The only big problem was remodeling the home when Wetherholt's family outgrew it. According to Wetherholt, remodeling earth-shelters is not an easy proposition. After 25 years or living underground, however, he removed the dirt from the roof and built a house on top of the existing underground home. Today, he lives in a much bigger conventional home on the same sit with a wonderfully constructed daylight basement.

Where Do We Go From Here?

The future of underground living can only get better as more people come to an awareness of the many benefits and rewards inherent in this type of living. Though certain practical constraints like financing and resale value still limit the production of these types of homes, it has been shown that they offer a very attractive and comfortable way to live. Underground home subdivisions and developments in England, as well as the creative efforts of people like those mentioned in the case studies of this book, may foreshadow a future where people think of underground living as more of the standard than the unusual. My personal vision of people's homes in the futures has always included more underground dwellings: homes that are extremely energy efficient and comfortable and homes which blend seamlessly and beautifully into the natural landscape.

A Word in Closing

Writing this book about earth-sheltered home has been a great joy to me. In the course of researching and writing about underground homes. I have been very fortunate to talk with many interesting and amazing people. I have even made a few new friends. The community involved with earth-shelter construction is a very tight knit group of people. It involves organizations who really love what they are doing and share this love and enthusiasm with anyone with whom they come into contact. For the most part I have found this group of people to be very friendly and helpful.

Clearly they recognize that the topic of underground construction is new to most people. There having been very few new good books on the subject, most of the population remains very uneducated on the topic. Most of these people recognize that getting people excited and enthusiastic about building or living in their own earth-shelter home takes patience and persistence. Most of all it takes a sharing of the passion they have found in the subject matter. Their passion for the idea is something you rarely see in anything. With this I can only see the ideas becoming more popular in the future.

What was started as a journey of discovering from curiosity over the pit homes of Native Americans in the Northwest lead down a road of many twists and turns. This journey of discovery lead us from the ancient earth rock shelters of Skara Brae to the modern underground mansion of William (Bill) Gates, III. Along the way, you learned about underground missile silo homes and the opal mine homes of Coober Pedy. You also heard about the 40 million people in China who do not consider living underground unusual at all.

Through it all, my respect for these interesting and marvelous structures was only increased. I have gained a marvelous admiration for the many innovative pioneers who have stretched our knowledge and expertise in a way of living that is both ancient and in some ways very modern.

I have many people I would like to thank for providing valuable information and helping me to clarify and explain some the finer points of earth-shelter building. All have provided extremely valuable help making the topic easier to understand to both the layman and the seasoned homebuilder. Many of these people worked very hard and helped by providing information for this book. This made the reading both more interesting and more enjoyable. Most of all, I would like to thank you the reader for taking the time to read my book about earth-sheltered homes. I hope the reading was both enjoyable and educational for you. If you are really interested in the topic, I would encourage you to continue learning and exploring it through the many writing and internet resources described in the back of the book. In closing, I wish you the best of luck with all your endeavors.

Appendix A

Sample Material List

CUST NO	JOB NO	PURCHASE ORDER	REFERENCE	TERMS	CLERK	DATE 10/14/09	TIME

SOLD TO:		SHIP TO:	
	MAJOR CONTRACTOR DISCOUNT CUST		MARINE FLOAT SERVICES NW BOB 360) 621-3113

EXP DATE: 10/18/09   DOC# 567847
SLSPR: 22 SCOTT KNUTSEN
TAX: 1BO 1BREMERTON1801   ST. 567847

LN#	SHIPPED	ORDERED	DESCRIPTION	SKU	UNITS	PRICE/PER	EXT.
1							
2	20	PC	2X10 20'	21020002	20	26.53/PC	530.78
3			MICROPRO				
4	26	PC	2X7 12'	2812002	26	12.48/PC	324.48
5			MIROPRO				
6	2	PC	4X10 20' TRTD	28100002	22	10.04/PC	220.9
7	3	PC	4X10 12' TRTD	41020TP	2	65.77/PC	131.55
8	1	PC	4X10 10' TRTD	41012TP	3	39.96/PC	118.4
9	16	PC	2X6 10'	41010TP	1	3.99/PX	32.97
10			MICROPRO				
11							
12							
13							
14	72	EA	4X8	261000D2	16	3.99/EA	287.28
15			CHEMONITE				
16			TREATED				
17			NON-STOCK				
18	60	PCC	2X6 12' KD	3	72	6.06/PC	363.9
19							
20	1	EA	TREE ISLAND	5	60	54.25/EA	54.25

X _____
RECEIVED BY

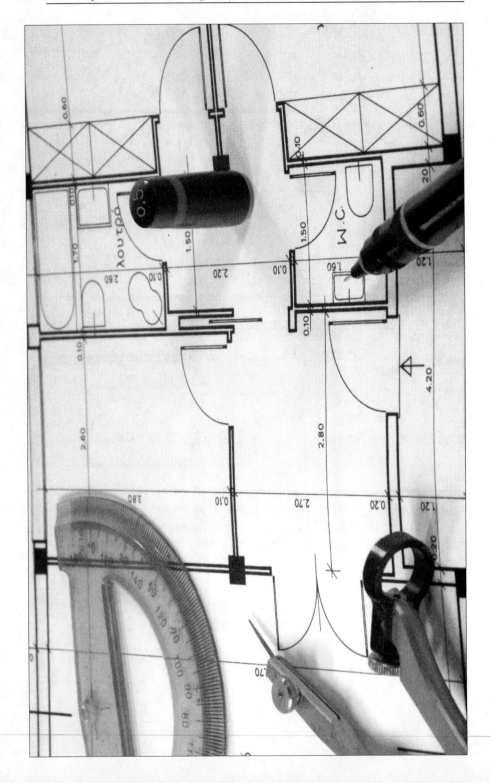

Appendix B

Typicial Home Design Plan

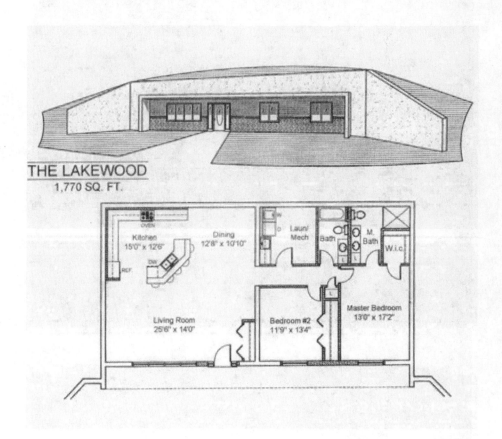

THE LAKEWOOD
1,770 SQ. FT.

Kitchen
15'0" x 12'6"

Dining
12'8" x 10'10"

Laun/
Mech

Bath

M.
Bath

W.i.c.

OVEN

REF

DW

Living Room
25'6" x 14'0"

Bedroom #2
11'9" x 13'4"

Master Bedroom
13'0" x 17'2"

Courtesy Earth Shelter Technology, Inc.

Appendix C

Sample Construction Contract

(For guidance only. Change to incorporate specifics of your project)
Original Document – courtesy of **www.dhca.state.vt.us/VCDP/ GMG/WORD/CONSTRUC.doc**

This agreement is made this <date> by and between <CONTRACTOR>, <ADDRESS>(hereinafter "Contractor") and <OWNER OF CONTRACT AND ADDRESS> (hereinafter "Owner").

WITNESSETH
Note: This section lays out the legal requirements of both parties entering into a contract

The owner does hereby employ the Contractor to do all the work and provide all the materials, tools, machinery and supervision necessary for the construction of a <DESCRIPTION OF WORK> in the <SITE>, the total sum of <AMOUNT>, all in accordance with the drawings, and specifications which are attached hereto as Exhibit ___ and expressly incorporated herein by reference and made a part hereof. Reference is made to an accompanying contract with <SUBCONTRACTOR, WHERE APPLICABLE>

which will be <INSERT A DESCRIPTION OF THE ACTIVITY> associated with this project.

The Contractor shall commence the work to be performed within ___ days from the date of the Notice to Proceed, and shall complete the work ___ days thereafter, or by <DATE>, whichever comes later, time being of the essence of this contract.

The Contractor shall carry liability insurance with the limits of <AMOUNT> for injury to or death of one person, <AMOUNT> for injuries or death suffered in one accident and <AMOUNT> property damage and Workman's Compensation insurance and shall provide Owner with proof of such insurance.

Hold Harmless
Note: This section protects the owner from contactors' liabilities
The Contractor agrees to defend, indemnify and hold the owner harmless from any liability or claim for damage because of bodily injury, death, property damage, sickness, disease or loss and expense arising from the Contractors' negligence in the performance of the construction Contract. Each Contractor and subcontractor is acting in the capacity of an independent Contractor with respect to the Owner. The Contractor further agrees to protect, defend and indemnify the Owner from any claims by laborers, subcontractors or materialmen for unpaid work or labor performed or materials supplied in connection with the Construction Contract

Assignment of Contract
Note: This section keeps the contractor from assigning the contract to someone else.

The contractor agrees not to assign the Construction Contract without the written consent of the Owner.

Change Orders
Note: This is a very important section that determines how any change to the work or change orders will be handled.

The Contractor agrees not to make any changes in the schedule of work, design, or of the specifications without written authorization by the Owner.

Lien Waivers
The Contractor shall protect, defend and indemnify the Owner from any claims for unpaid work, labor or materials.

General Guarantee
Note: Most states have a legal requirement of a warranty from a contractor for 1 to 2 years from completion of work regardless of the contract requirements. If you want a longer warranty it needs to be listed in the contract.

The Contractor shall remedy any defect due to faulty material or workmanship and pay for any damage to other work resulting therefrom which shall appear within the period of one year from final payment. Further, the Contractor will furnish Owner with all manufacturer's and supplier's written guarantees and warranties covering materials and equipment furnished under this Contract.

Permits and Codes
Note: This keeps your construction legal. You can also specify permits are to be obtained by the contractor.

The Owner shall obtain all necessary building permits, including those required by the <MUNICIPALITY>, <STATE AGENCY>, and Act 250 as applicable. The Contractor will secure at his/her own expense any other necessary permits and licenses required to do the work and will comply with all building and code regulations and ordinances whether or not covered by the specifications and drawings for the work.

Work Performance

1) The Contractor shall protect all work adjacent to the Contract site from any damage resulting from the work of the Contractor and shall repair or replace any damaged work at his/her own expense.
2) The Contractor shall replace and put in good condition any existing conditions damaged in carrying out the contract.
3) The Contractor shall take all precautions to protect persons from injury and unnecessary interference or inconvenience.
4) The Contractor shall conduct his activities in a business like manner and adhere to the reasonable wishes of the Owner in relation to his working schedule.

Condition of Premises

Note: Make sure your contract has this clause or the contractor does not have to clean–up.

The Contractor agrees to keep the premises clean and orderly and to remove all debris as needed during the hours of work in order to maintain work conditions which do not cause health or safety hazards.

Use of Utilities

The Owner shall permit the Contractor to use, at no cost, power and water necessary to the carrying out and completion of the work.

Inspection

Note: This clause allows you and others to inspect the contractor work.

The Owner shall have the right to inspect all work performed under this contract. As well it shall be a condition of this contract that all work that needs to be inspected or tested and certified by the engineer as a condition of the Dept. of Environmental Conservation Permit, (or other State agency), or inspected and certified by the local health officer, shall be done at each necessary stage before further construction can continue. All inspection and certification will be done at the Owner's expense. Failure to follow this requirement will be grounds for termination of the contract.

Right to Stop Work

Note: This clause gives you a way to get the contractor's attention if you are having problems with the construction.

If the Contractor fails to correct defective work or persistently fails to supply materials or equipment in accordance with the Contract Documents, the Owner may order the Contractor to stop the work, or any portion thereof, until the cause for such order has been eliminated.

Payment Schedule

Note: This part of the contact lays out how the contractor will be paid for the work. Make sure you are always holding enough money to ensure the proper performance of the contract.

Payments for work shall be as follows:

Payments shall be disbursed based on the attached schedule of values. Within three days of notification by the Contractor of each stage of completion, the Owner or its designee will inspect and approve the work, or request any necessary adjustments in the work. The Owner agrees to make payments to the Contractor within ten days of approving work.

Contract Security
Note: This section provides security from the contractor that the work will be done correctly. Not many projects require more than a state bond. Additional bonding or other pervasion can cost you additional money, up to 1.5 percent of the cost of the project.

Contractor shall furnish bonds covering the faithful performance of the Contract and the payment of all obligations related thereto and as required in the instructions to bidders or elsewhere in this Contract.

Contract Security (In lieu of conventional performance and payment bonds)
Contractor shall grant to Owner a mortgage on certain property in <LOCATION> as set forth in Exhibit ___. The mortgage shall secure the performance by Contractor of all of Contractor's obligations under this agreement including, but not limited to, completion of the work for the Contract's price; indemnification of Owner from claims as set forth in this agreement; Contractor's general guarantee of materials and workmanship, and any special or consequential damages to which Owner may be entitled as a result of breach of this Contract by Contractor. The mortgage shall further secure the payment of any award to Owner pursuant

to arbitration as provided herein. Contractor acknowledges that this mortgage is being accepted by Owner in lieu of a conventional performance and payment bond with a commercial surety, as well as Owner's agreement not to require retainage during construction. Contractor further acknowledges that the Owner has a limited ability to complete the Contract on its own in the event of Contractor's default, and that the Owner may freely assign the mortgage and any interests it may have as mortgagee. Owner agrees that the Contractor shall be entitled to a discharge of the mortgage one year from the date that the final payment for the completion of the work is made, or ___ days following payment in full by Contractor of any award to Owner pursuant to arbitration pending at the end of the one year period, whichever occurs later.

Liquidated Damages
Note: Most residential construction contracts do not have liquidated damage provisions. These make the contractor pay for any delays on the project beyond a certain point and are good to have if you are under severe time constraints. Most contractors do not like them for obvious reasons and usually charge extra for them to cover possible liability.

Contractor hereby agrees to commence work under this contract within <DAYS> days of the Notice to Proceed and to fully complete the project within <DAYS> consecutive calendar days thereafter. Contractor further agrees to pay as liquidated damages, the sum of <AMOUNT> for each consecutive calendar day thereafter. These damages shall not apply, should unforeseeable causes beyond the control and without the fault or negligence of the Contractor cause delays in the completion of this project.

Taxes

Note: This is an important clause to have because if your contractor does not pay taxes and goes out of business you are sometimes liable to pay them.

The Owner hereby agrees to supply the Contractor with its tax exempt number for relief from the sales tax on purchase of materials, if applicable.

Arbitration

Note: Arbitration clauses can save you plenty of money by keeping contracting disputes out of court. Instead they are handled by a much cheaper mediation system.

1) All claims, disputes, and other matters in question arising out of, or relating to, the Contract Documents or the breach thereof, except for claims which have been waived by the making and acceptance of final payment, shall be decided by Arbitration in accordance with the construction Industry Arbitration Rules of the American Arbitration Association (or other arbitration rules). This agreement to arbitrate shall be specifically enforceable under the prevailing arbitration law. The award rendered by the arbitrators shall be final, and judgement may be entered upon it in any court having jurisdiction thereof. Any award shall provide for payment within 30 days of the date of the award.

2) Notice of the demand for arbitration shall be filed in writing with the other party to the CONTRACT DOCUMENTS and with the <ARBITER=Notice of the demand for arbitration shall be filed in writing with the other party to the CONTRACT DOCUMENTS and with the

<ARBITER the award.he award.ch have been waived by the

3) The Contractor will carry on the work and maintain the progress schedule during any arbitration proceedings, unless otherwise mutually agreed in writing.

Conflict of Interest

No person who is an employee, agent, consultant, officer, or elected or appointed official of the <MUNICIPALITY> or other pertinent party may obtain a personal or financial interest or benefit form, or have an interest in, this contract or the proceeds hereunder, either for themselves or for those with whom they have family or business ties, during their tenure or for one year thereafter, if they exercise or have exercised any functions or responsibilities with respect to the program or are in a position to participate in a decision making process or gain inside information with regard to the program.

This Contract shall be construed under the laws of the State of _____ and may be modified or amended only by a written instrument executed by both the Owner and the Contractor.

IN WITNESS WHEREOF, THE OWNER AND THE CONTRACTOR HAVE EXECUTED THIS CONTRACT AS OF THE DATE FIRST WRITTEN ABOVE.

_____ CONTRACTOR NAME

_____ OWNER NAME

_____AUTHORIZED SIGNATURE

Glossary

Atrium: A rectangular open patio around which a house is constructed

Berm: A mound or wall of earth piled in a slope again a foundation wall

Competition factor: Using competition between several pricing sources to drive the cost down

Concrete blowout: This occurs when the weight of concrete causes a failure in the forming system

Conduction: The transfer of heat or energy through a medium

Contoured: Area of different elevation

Contractor: Business that agrees to provide a construction service for a set price

Convection: The transfer of heat by circulating currents

Cost of ownership or total cost of ownership (TCO): The initial cost plus maintenance expenses

Curing: The process of getting harder or drying

Curing agent: A chemical that promotes more rapid curing

Dried-in: The waterproofing of a building specifically after the roof is installed completely

Earth bags: Plastic bags filled with earth used in construction like sand bags

Earth-sheltered: An erection that utilized the earth or dirt as a part of its structure

Earthship: Construction methodology that utilizes scrap material such as cans or tires filled with earth

Elevation: Height above a grade level

Epoxy cement: Concrete that has been supplemented with an epoxy compound for strength

Excavation contractor: Contractor who does the excavation, piling, and backfilling on a property

Finished electrical: Electrical final trim, which includes light fixtures, outlet cover plates, and switch plates

Finished plumbing: Installation of final plumbing fixtures such as sinks, toilets, and showers

Fly-ash: Volcanic ash material added to concrete to improve its strength without adding more cement

Footings: Concrete structure which transfers the building loads from the foundation to the ground

Form bowing: Movement of concrete forms due to concrete pressures

Glulam beams: Composite wood beam made by gluing smaller pieces of wood together

Grade stamp: A lumber mill's stamp on lumber cut which specifies the type and grade of lumber produced

Gunite: Dry concrete mortar used in shotcrete

I beams: Steel beam manufactured in the shape of an I

In-floor heating: Radiant heating done by laying piping through or under a floor system

In-ground construction: Earth shelter construction where the site is excavated, the home is constructed, and the structure is covered with earth

In-hill construction Earth shelter construction similar to a cave

Lifecycle costs: The cost of something from the time it is built until it is no longer usable

Marginalized land: Land which for some reason or another is not fully usable

Means unit pricing: The price or time to do a unit of work as specified by the Means Construction Data Company

Mil thickness: One mil is 0.001 inches in thickness

Murphy's law: "If something can go wrong, it will"

Passive solar heating: Using the sun to heat a home without any mechanical means

Perk test: Testing the porosity of the soil by seeing how well it drains water over time

Pit-home: Native American earth-shelter consisting of a pit covered with logs, bark, and earth

Post and beam framing: Framing which uses posts and beams for its superstructure (same as timber framing)

Post-tensioned: Concrete precast structures that are held together by tensioned wires after they are placed

Precast panels: Concrete construction panels that are manufactured in a concrete precasting company

Property covenants: Rules or legal requirements that come with a certain piece of property

Reverse print: Blueprints that should be framed backwards from the way the plans are drawn

Rough electrical: Installation of the wiring and electrical connection boxes prior to covering framing

Rough plumbing: Installation of the supply, waste, and vent piping prior to covering the framing

R-Value: A measurement of the insulation capacity of a material

Screed: A strip of material used to level concrete

Septic drain: Land area used to drain septic waste

Shimming: A thin tapered or wedge-shaped piece of material used to level something

Shotcrete: The application of gunite, mortar, or concrete with air pressure through a hose

Southern exposure: Facing a structure to the south so that it collects more sunlight

Stick framing: Framing a structure with wood 2 x 4 or 2 x 6 studs and standard wood components

Stucco: Durable cement and sand or plaster material used to finish the exterior

Subsurface conditions: Conditions below the ground that are not generally visible

Sweat equity: Using your own labor to save money and build up equity in the construction

Test cylinder: Cylinder of concrete 4inches in diameter by 8″ high that is poured and crushed tested later

Test ping: Test pinging involves a small pin that "pings" or hits the concrete. The strength of the concrete can then be determined by how deeply the pin penetrates the concrete

Thermal mass: Mass that absorbs and holds heat

Timber framing: See Post and beam framing

Transit level: Device used to level to points by using a measured rod and a small telescope

Wood heat   Heating with a wood stove

Bibliography

Web Resources

http://architecture.about.com/od/greenarchitecture/g/earth-shelter.htm

www.bobvila.com/HowTo_Library/Earth_Sheltered_Houses-Energy_Efficiency-A1615.html

http://buzzle.com/articles/underground-homes-wave-of-the-future.html

http://daviscaves.com/index.shtml

http://earthshelteredhome.com

http://ellerman79.tripod.com

http://earthshelter.com

http://earthshelters.com

http://earthshelteredtech.com

http://energysavers.gov/your_home/designing_remodeling/index.cfm/mytopic=10100

http://villageearth.org/pages/Projects/Pine_Ridge/SustainableHousing/Earth.htm

http://freespace.virgin.net/andrew.seccull/earthsh.htm#DISSERTATION%20SUMMARY

Book Resources

Carmody, J. and R. Sterling. 1985. *Earth Sheltered Housing Design*. 2nd ed. Van Nostrand Reinhold.

Hall , Loretta. 2004. *Underground Buildings – More Than Meets the Eye*. Quill Driver Books. Sanger CA.

Hunter, Kaki and Donald Kiffmeyer. 2004. *Earthbag Building*. New Society Publishers. Gabriola Island, BC Canada

Kennedy, Joseph F, Smith, Michael G., Wenek, Catherine et al. 2002. *Natural Buildings*. New Society Publishers. Gabriola Island, BC Canada

Kern, Ken & Barbara, Jane & Otis Mullan. 1982. *The Earth-Sheltered Owners-Built Home* .Mullan Press/Owner-Builders Publications.

Mazria, E. 1979. *The Passive Solar Energy Book*. Rodale Press.

Oehler, Mike. 2007.*The Earth-Sheltered Solar Greenhouse Book*. Mole Publishing Company. Bonners Ferry, Idaho

Oehler, Mike. 1997. *The $50 & Up Underground House Book*. Mole Publishing Company. Bonners Ferry, Idaho

Pugliese, Michael. 2006. *The Homeowners Guide to Mold*. Reed Construction Data Inc. Kingston, MA

Roy, Rob. 2006. *Earth–Sheltered Houses*. New Society Publishers. Gabriola Island, BC Canada

Roy, Rob. 2003.*Cordwood Building: The State of the Art*. New Society Publishers. Gabriola Island, BC Canada

Ruiz, Frenando. 2005. *Building an Affordable House – Trade Secrets to High-Value Low-Cost Construction*. The Taunton Press. Newtown, CT.

Sterling, R., W. Farnan, and J. Carmody. 1982. *Earth-Sheltered Residential Design Manual*. Van Nostrand Reinhold.

Terman, M. 1985. *Earth-Sheltered Housing: Principles in Practice*. Van Nostrand Reinhold, 209 pages.

Vale, Robert & Brenda. *The New Autonomous House – Design & Planning for Sustainability*. Thames & Hudson. New York, NY

Wells, Malcolm. 1998. *The Earth-Sheltered House*. Chealsea Green Publishing. White River Junction VT.

Author Biography

Robert Alan McConkey is a native of the Pacific Northwest where he grew up with a passionate interest in science and business. After getting an undergraduate degree in Zoology and Oceanography from the University of Washington, he went on to manage a small homebuilding and remodeling company in the Seattle area. An active member of the Kitsap County Home Builders Association, McConkey served as a national director to the Home Builders Association in the early 1980s. Later he owned and operated a marine construction company that built concrete and wood floating docks.

Robert is still active in his marine construction and maintenance business and works part-time as a freelance writer and business consultant. He currently teaches several online courses on e-commerce and is a published writer and poet. He has a master's degree in business and holds a teaching certificate for High School level math and science. His wife Helen and two grown children, Andrew and Kendra, enjoy an active life in the Pacific Northwest that includes boating, scuba diving, running, and cycling.

Index